Extra Innings

Sport and Society

Series Editors
Benjamin G. Rader
Randy Roberts

A list of books in the series
appears at the end of this book.

Extra Innings

Writing on Baseball

Richard Peterson

Foreword by Eliot Asinof

BRIGGS SACRAMENTO P C. L.

University of Illinois Press
Urbana and Chicago

Manufactured in the United States of America

1 2 3 4 5 C P 5 4 3 2 1

∞ This book is printed on acid-free paper.

Library of Congress Cataloging-in-Publication Data
Peterson, Richard F.
Extra innings : writing on baseball / Richard Peterson ;
foreword by Eliot Asinof.
p.   cm. — (Sport and society)
Includes bibliographical references and index.
ISBN 0-252-02647-0 (cl. : acid-free paper)
ISBN 0-252-06960-9 (pbk. : acid-free paper)
1. American literature—History and criticism.
2. Baseball stories, American—History and criticism.
3. Baseball—United States—Historiography.
4. Baseball in literature. I. Title. II. Series.
PS169.B36P48   2001
810.9'355—dc21   00-011381

◆ ◆

For Anita

And in memory of Frank Peterson

Contents

Foreword

Eliot Asinof

Pound the pocket of your baseball glove as you read Richard Peterson's leadoff essay, "Soaking Clete Boyer," and get ready to field the rest of the essays in *Extra Innings*. Yes, I was there in Cooperstown, standing with Peterson's beautiful wife, Anita, watching that chaotic demonstration of the ancient game of townball. I was too sensible to participate and would later tease Boyer for his folly to get soaked. Above all, we should thank the memory of the distinguished Henry Chadwick for establishing the rules of baseball that would put townball into the dustbin of our history.

I can also testify that Boyer was indeed a presence at the subsequent dinner, fortified by Old Slugger and a mutually courtly attention to Peterson's wife. I would add that when Boyer was introduced as "perhaps the best glove in N.Y. Yankee history," I took exception to the superlative (mostly in deference to my memories of Craig Nettles) by calling out a qualification: "*one* of the best!" It was worth a few laughs. A few moments later, when I was introduced as the author of "perhaps the best baseball book ever written," Boyer saw fit to call out "*one* of the best!" which, of course, brought down the house. I might add that I cherish the photo of Boyer's embracing me at that moment, taken by none other than Anita Peterson.

On the serious side, Peterson's essays are rich with the reflections of an extremely well-read baseball fan as he slices away the myths and distortions of baseball's bizarre history. Throughout these essays, Peterson stakes his case for the purity and sensibility of baseball's vast literature out of respect for what the great game should mean to us all. He sets the record straight with critiques of tomes by A. G. Spalding (re: Abner Doubleday) and Albert Spink (re: Henry Chadwick). (If Cooperstown has become a national shrine, it's a myth that baseball was first played there.) In another essay he bemoans much of the fiction that deals with baseball as fantasy, railing at the mythmaking, the fables, the lack of realism. Childish plots that end up in fantasy movies. Too many fields of dreams and angels dancing in the outfields. He hungers for the nitty gritty. The overload of trivia insults him. One by one, he takes on writers of baseball fiction: W. P. Kinsella, Robert Coover, Philip Roth, Mark Harris, myself. He properly demands a more realistic approach to our work. He especially criticizes recent novelists for our failure to deal adequately with racial problems. What better theme to explain the segregated horrors of pre–Jackie Robinson years than the harsh fact that white ballplayers battled all attempts to integrate, not only for the usual reasons of racial bigotry but out of fear of losing their jobs? It had never been a secret that black ballplayers were great. Years before Robbie, everyone had heard of Satchel Paige and Josh Gibson and Cool Papa Bell. Nor have race problems in professional ball, even after integration, been explored. Why haven't these horrors been written from a black player's point of view, the way Richard Wright or Ralph Ellison wrote of their own youths? Instead, the celebrated documentary by Ken Burns gives us the gentle articulate sweetness of the black Buck O'Neal, whose smile denied the rage of his colleagues. The same America had viciously badgered Henry Aaron with death threats as he approached Babe Ruth's all-time record. Indeed, the entire history of baseball literally throbs with exclusions because of race hate, anti-Semitism, small-minded bigotry. In my own mini-experience as a prewar minor leaguer, I was constantly bench-jockeyed as "kike," "Hitler's boy," or simply "Jewboy." Once, an umpire named Reagan called an eye-high strike on me, whereupon a hometown voice bellowed "Reagan, you kike!" which, of course, was the last word in absurdity.

In the end, Peterson forgives us writers for our failures as he contemplates writing his own true piece of baseball fiction, which may, quite possibly, remain out of reach for us all. The magic of baseball is simply too loaded with hard-ass complexities, too subtle, too evasive.

I put the book down, still pounding the pocket of my old glove.

Preface

Extra Innings begins with "Soaking Clete Boyer," a mostly truthful essay about an exhausted university department chair who believes he can save his soul by going to Cooperstown and visiting the Hall of Fame. The collection ends with "How to Write a True Baseball Story," a mostly made-up story about a delusional university professor, no longer a department chair, who loses his mind because he takes baseball, especially baseball writing, far too seriously.

The nine essays in between begin with the word of baseball and the way that baseball's writers have spread the word by glorifying the game and mythologizing its players. In narratives ranging from personal essays and oral histories to biographies, histories, and fiction, baseball writers have generated a narrative tradition, replete with a myth of origin, a fabled past, and a pantheon of baseball immortals.

After two essays on baseball's narrative tradition, *Extra Innings* looks specifically at the writing of baseball histories and baseball fiction. There are companion pieces on the first attempts, by Albert G. Spalding and Alfred H. Spink, to write the first standard history of baseball, and the more modern attempts to mix dream and reality into standard and academic histories. There are also companion pieces on baseball fiction's short and long game and the way that short stories and novels often treat baseball as the stuff of moral romances and magical realism or confuse the realities of the game with baseball stereotypes.

The last three essays in *Extra Innings* follow baseball writing through the second half of the twentieth century. The cluster begins with the influence of Jackie Robinson on the serious or adult baseball novel and examines why racial discrimination hasn't been treated more directly and realistically in baseball fiction. There is also an essay that looks at the recent trend in postmodern baseball writing of seeing the game as a faltering enterprise, no longer capable of sustaining itself as the national pastime because of greedy ownership and selfish ballplayers. The last essay, noting the absence of baseball books on the Modern Library's list of the one hundred best novels and one hundred best nonfiction books of the twentieth century, offers nine baseball books as worthy candidates for the century's best books.

Taken together, the essays and stories in *Extra Innings* travel the course of baseball history from its rowdy nineteenth-century days to its contentious, fractured present. In their travels, they also provide a commentary, in form and content, on the way baseball writing—from personal and historical essays to realistic and fantastic stories—has shaped our understanding and misunderstanding of the game. In writing these essays and stories, I've realized all over again how important baseball has been in my life, but I've also learned how much of what I enjoy about the game has been handed down to me through oral and written history. My hope is that the writing in *Extra Innings* reflects the joy I've experienced as a baseball fan and the enjoyment I've gained as a baseball reader from the books that have elevated the game of our youth into a national pastime.

Though an academic by training and career, I've tried to write my essays on baseball writing with a minimum of critical apparatus. I see these essays as a conversation with other writers rather than a critical text and the quotations as part of our conversation.

Acknowledgments

I want to thank the organizers of the Cooperstown Symposium on Baseball and American Culture, the Indiana State Conference on Baseball in Literature and Culture, and the annual meetings of the Society of American Baseball Research and the Sports Literature Association for the opportunity to try out my own baseball writings.

I owe many personal debts to those who were indispensable in helping with the research for the book and to those who read and offered important advice and criticism about the writing of individual essays and stories. Tim Wiles and Corey Seeman of the National Hall of Fame Library were wonderful in providing valuable research and directing me to other sources. I am also grateful to Steve Gietschier of *The Sporting News* for his help with the Spink essay. My list of those who encouraged the writing of other essays and stories includes Lee Gutkind, Kent Haruf, Jerry Klinkowitz, Don Johnson, Chris Messenger, Tim Morris, and Jim Shepard.

I want to express my special gratitude to Eliot Asinof for agreeing to write the foreword to the book and for his friendship over the past few years. I wish to give special thanks to Eileen Glass, whose professionalism, good cheer, and understanding made all the difference in preparing the manuscript. And, finally, my loving thanks to my road companion, baseball buddy, and wife, Anita Peterson, who helped me find my way to places like Cooperstown and made sure I spoke up and didn't slouch when I gave my papers.

◆ ◆

Earlier versions of all or part of several essays were published elsewhere:

"Only Fairy Tales: Baseball Fiction's Short Game," *Aethlon* 14 (Spring 1997): 63–70

"How to Write a True Baseball Story," *Elysian Fields Quarterly* 15 (Fall 1998): 10–16

"Jackie Robinson and the Serious Baseball Novel," in *The Cooperstown Symposium on Baseball and American Culture 1997* (Jefferson, N.C.: McFarland, 2000), 215–26

"In Defense of Baseball Books," *Chicago Tribune*, June 4, 2000, 3.

Extra Innings

◆ 1 ◆

Soaking Clete Boyer:
A True Cooperstown Story

My travels to Cooperstown began with good intentions. I was enduring an afternoon of discontent in the middle of my ninth and, as it turned out, final year of chairing my English department, when I came across an ad in *The Chronicle of Higher Education* for the Seventh Cooperstown Symposium on Baseball and American Culture. Unlike Ishmael, I didn't have the option, in landlocked southern Illinois, of curing the damp, drizzly November of my soul by sailing around the watery part of the world. So I answered the call for papers and began an adventure that would end up, like the quest for the white whale, in deception, scandal, horror, and tragedy. What began as a journey by a weary, aging academic to restore the boyhood innocence of his soul became a harrowing descent, in four stages, into a baseball heart of darkness where he gradually learned the truth about Cooperstown: its carefully buried secrets, its shameful abuse of history, and its insidious seduction of loyalty and honor.

What you are about to read, however, is not another one of those Stephen Jay Gould or George Will exposés on the myth of Cooperstown. Most baseball fans, whether or not they have been to the Hall of Fame, know something about A. G. Spalding's claim that Abner Doubleday invented baseball in a Cooperstown cow pasture in 1839. And some may even know that, shortly after the Mills Commission came out in 1907 with its trumped up report in support of Spalding's claim, prominent baseball editors and writers of that time like Alfred H. Spink, founder of *The Sporting News,* were already calling the Doubleday story with the Cooperstown flavor a fake. Neither is my Cooperstown story a thinly veiled attempt to mimic baseball solon Bill James on the politics of Cooperstown and who should or should not be in the Hall of Fame. The scandal I uncovered has nothing to do with whether or not Joe Jackson, Pete Rose, or Bill Mazeroski belongs in Cooperstown. There is a great deal of irony in the Hall of Fame displaying Shoeless Joe Jackson's spikes and Bill Mazeroski's glove, while Baseball has banned the one for his ignorance and penalizes the other for making Mickey Mantle cry. But Jackson and Mazeroski already have their fiercely loyal advocates, and even Pete Rose may get into the Hall of Fame if he ever learns a modicum of diplomacy, or at least learns to keep his mouth shut and let others speak for him.

The myth of Cooperstown and Hall of Fame politics were no more than distant rumblings when my wife and I left for my first baseball symposium in June 1995. Nothing, not the pessimistic title of Leonard Koppett's keynote address—"Baseball as We Knew It: Never Again"— or the dark clouds from the previous year's baseball strike and the cancellation of the World Series, could dampen my spirit. I wasn't even that disturbed by the scheduling of my session in the Billiard Room of the Masonic Lodge rather than in the National Baseball Library or the Hall of Fame. It's not easy presenting a paper on the dream narratives of baseball fiction when your audience is scattered around a billiard table, but I was a rookie at the symposium and grateful for the chance to talk about baseball after haggling all spring with my dean about budget, staffing, and class sizes.

I enjoyed the symposium, but I have to admit that I spent most of my time in Cooperstown playing hooky from sessions to wander through the Hall of Fame or shop with my wife for memorabilia and souvenirs. For the middle-aged baseball fan, Cooperstown is America's Mecca. Once you enter the red-bricked Hall of Fame building with its impressive colonial design and Ionic columns and pass through the green turnstiles, you become a part of the religion and history of baseball. While there are enough special rooms, alcoves, and displays to dazzle and eventually confound the sensibilities of the most ardent fan, the heart's core of the building is the Hall of Fame Gallery, and its pulse is the baseball time line. All a baseball fan needs to do is worship at the gallery, with its plaques commemorating baseball's immortals, then stroll along the time line, with its historical artifacts honoring baseball's great events and teams, to understand the spiritual and emotional appeal of baseball as America's national game.

As my wife and I ate delightfully greasy food at the Bullpen Café and the Shortstop Café, waved our Visa card like Wonderboy at a gallery of souvenir shops, and rested reverentially in the bleachers of Abner Doubleday Field, I had no idea how close we were to one of the buried secrets of Cooperstown and how narrow was to be our escape from scandal. Because I had to leave the symposium a day early to get back for the opening of the summer semester, I was to miss the traditional townball game and the memorial ceremony for baseball historian Harold Seymour, thereby delaying my first encounter with the darker side of Cooperstown until the following year.

If I'd never returned to Cooperstown I would have been left with a romantic vision of glowing plaques and that classic Norman Rockwell painting, of bottleneck bats and fingerless gloves, of ghostly figures moving about in the twilight of Doubleday Field. But my wife and I did go back—she claimed Cooperstown had saved my health and our marriage—and therein hangs my tale. Our first visit was wonderful, but I fully expected our second trip to be even better. We found an inn with no telephones or television sets in its rooms and made a reservation to stay for the entire symposium. My paper on postmodern baseball narratives, titled "Barbarians at the Plate," was timely, contro-versial, and a contender, I thought, for a call-up to the National Base-ball Library or the Hall of Fame. The keynote speaker was to be the master of magical realism, W. P. Kinsella, and I was going to play town-ball on some timeless field of dreams.

The first warning sign that there was more to Cooperstown than I'd ever dreamed was the scheduling of my paper in the Masonic Lodge again. I'd hoped to move up, but the organizers of the symposium had reassigned me to another year with that damn billiard table. The sec-ond warning came after we got to Cooperstown and I discovered that W. P. Kinsella hated me. It was nothing personal—Kinsella hated all academic critics. At his keynote, when asked what he had against crit-ics, Kinsella proclaimed he actually had the heart of a critic—in a jar on his writing desk.

The billiard table and Kinsella's jar, however, were merely tremors, minor disturbances, as I ate in the usual cafés, bought even more sou-venirs, gloried in the inner sanctum of the Hall of Fame, and gazed out with my mind's eye over the infield dirt and green grass of Dou-bleday Field. It wasn't until I played townball on the last evening of the symposium that I began to suspect I was becoming involved in something insidious to my baseball soul. What should have been a delightful excursion into the romance of baseball's past became the sinister turning point in my Cooperstown travels.

On the surface, or at least on the surface of the pasture we used at Cooperstown, playing townball seemed like the perfect ending for a symposium on baseball. The townball game, organized and played according to the rules first adopted on May 13, 1858, for the Massa-chusetts Game, has a wonderful spirit of democracy and fair play about it. Since everyone is invited to play, and that usually means each side will have about twenty players, the townball game has no racial, gen-der, or age barriers. At the beginning of the game the pasture is filled with a rich diversity of staketenders (infielders) and scouts (outfielders).

The thrower (pitcher), according to the rules, has to deliver the ball overhanded but at a slow speed and "in a manner calculated to assist the striker in hitting the ball." The striker (batter) stands between the first stake and the fourth, or home, stake and may request from the thrower where he prefers the ball delivered, since the thrower is "essentially a trigger to put the ball in play." With no balls and strikes and therefore no boring walks or embarrassing strikeouts, the fun begins when the striker puts the ball in play. And with no foul territory in townball, play is everywhere. Since the struck ball, if not caught on the fly, is thrown at runners to put them out, the runner, to avoid being "soaked" or "plugged," can run to any stake for safety or even head into the outfield or hide in the surrounding woods. With no walks or strikeouts, no foul balls or restrictive base lines, townball has infinite possibilities for delightful confusion and chaos, all played out within a gentlemanly spirit of cooperation and fun—or so I thought.

After listening to a long lecture on the rules of townball that confused the art of the timeless with the boredom of the endless, we finally got to play, but only after standing in line and counting off odd and even numbers. This random selection of teams seemed fair enough, but the uncanny result was that our team was made up almost exclusively of first-timers at townball, including the wives, sons, and daughters of participants. While we tried to organize ourselves, the other team took the field, and remarkably its players ran to set positions, including their thrower. What followed during the next hour was a townball debacle. As our team's thrower, I grooved pitch after pitch "to assist the striker in hitting the ball," but their thrower, despite our gentlemanly and occasional ladylike requests to lower his pitches, threw everything high, which we routinely popped up. On the field we resembled a Mack Sennett comedy, while the other team seemed to know exactly how to place the ball, run the stakes, and field their positions. The final score, though the umpire politely declared the game a tie, was so one-sided it gave new meaning to a townball soaking.

When I returned to Cooperstown for my third symposium, I brought with me my suspicion about the annual townball game. Just before

driving to Cooperstown I also received my first sensible shock about
the symposium after reading an article in *The National Pastime* written by that same thrower who refused to throw strikes at last year's
game. I discovered that after the townball game I missed two years ago
the participants attended a ceremony in which Harold Seymour's ashes
were scattered near first base at Abner Doubleday Field. Now I know
I shouldn't have been all that shocked or disturbed by the discovery.
After all, Professor Seymour, one of baseball's great historians, deserved
the honor, and most serious baseball fans, myself included, have often thought about having our ashes scattered over some hometown
ballpark. The only thing preventing me from making the request to
my wife is the knowledge that Three Rivers Stadium, the current home
of my beloved Pirates, has artificial turf, and my scattered ashes would
be sucked up into the belly of some Zamboni machine.

But discovering Harold Seymour was the answer, as the director of
the symposium had joked, to the question of who's on first, at least at
Doubleday Field, did unnerve me. It's one thing to imagine ghostly
ballplayers on a field of dreams, but staring out at a dirt infield and
knowing who's on first, wondering what's at second, and realizing I
don't know's at third is a whole different ballgame. I've always bought
into the notion of ballfields as green cathedrals, but Doubleday Field
had now become more of a gothic House of Usher than a baseball
shrine. I still paid my respects to the ancient ballpark, but I no longer
felt the urge to run around the basepaths as I had before.

Still, though Doubleday Field had lost its innocent charm and tak-
en on a funereal atmosphere, there was plenty of wonder and delight
left in Cooperstown to lure me back a third time. I had my doubts
about playing townball again, but the program for my third symposium was irresistible. Since the symposium was tied in with the Hall
of Fame's celebration of the fiftieth anniversary of the integration of
the Major Leagues, we were asked to present papers on the influence
of Jackie Robinson on American culture. As participants we were also
invited to attend the grand opening of the exhibit "Pride and Passion:

The African-American Baseball Experience." Instead of listening to a pessimistic Leonard Koppett deliver a doomsday address, we heard a passionate Joe Morgan plea for more minorities in baseball management and administration. Instead of waiting for an acerbic W. P. Kinsella to sign a copy of *Shoeless Joe,* my wife and I watched a generous Rachel Robinson, who had spoken earlier about her scholarship program, write a personal dedication in *Jackie Robinson: An Intimate Portrait,* while she wondered when she would have a chance to see her grandchildren again. At my third symposium I also reached my own personal moment of triumph, when I gave my paper on Jackie Robinson's influence on the adult baseball novel in the Bullpen Theatre of the Hall of Fame. I had finally escaped the Masonic Lodge and another round with the billiard table and made it to the Big Show.

Escaping townball, however, was another matter. After finishing my annual pilgrimage through the Hall of Fame Gallery, I found myself walking behind the thrower, two of his teammates from last year, and someone I hadn't seen before at the symposium. I overheard them urging their friend to play townball because they'd fix it so they'd be playing on the same team. All they had to do was stand in line, as they did every year, so that their cronies were all number twos, a number that now seemed singularly appropriate for what I was overhearing.

I felt like Nick Carraway after Jay Gatsby tells him Meyer Wolfsheim, modeled after the real-life gangster Arnold Rothstein, had fixed the 1919 World Series. What I heard staggered me. It never occurred to me that a handful of symposium participants could play with the faith of all the other symposiasts. I was actually walking behind townball conspirators, the Eddie Cicottes, Chick Gandils, and Swede Risbergs of the Cooperstown symposium. I now knew the fix was in at the townball game but, as I headed back to my inn, I didn't quite know what to do about it.

By the time my wife and I arrived at the townball game, I had decided not to say anything, partly because I feared that if I blew the whistle I might end up back at the Masonic Lodge with its infamous billiard table or even worse. Instead I was determined to pitch again to the symposium's team of ringers. I listened to the same lengthy town-ball sermon on the cow pasture, stood in line and made sure I wasn't a number two, and volunteered to be our team's thrower. Instead of grooving the ball to assist their strikers, I came up with something between Satchel Paige's hesitation pitch and Rip Sewell's blooper ball. Since all you need in townball is one out to retire the side, my strategy worked. We popped out, but they popped out too. Instead of a townball soaking, we had a pitcher's duel that turned a picnic outing into a fierce competition replete with arguments, taunting, and cheating—all those things that made baseball what it is today.

I'd like to tell you the good guys and a few gals—the true amateurs and innocents of the symposium—won the game in some heroic last time at bat, because that's the way true baseball stories are supposed to end. But when a thunderstorm moved in with lightning flashing across the Cooperstown early evening sky, we had no Robert Redford—Malamud's Roy Hobbs, unlike the Hollywood version, strikes out—to win the game with one magical blow. We left the field losers, but by only two tallies. Later, as my teammates and I drank a loser's amount of Old Slugger beer at a local inn, some of us vowed to return to Cooperstown next year and cleanse the annual townball game with a victory over the game's fixers and ringers.

By the time my wife and I drove back to Cooperstown for our fourth symposium, I'd already decided that a rigged townball game was not going to undermine my romance with the Hall of Fame. Besides the usual fun of talking baseball at the symposium, strolling through the souvenir shops, and visiting the Hall of Fame Museum and Library, I was bringing my own contribution to Cooperstown, copies of Eliot Asinof's *Man on Spikes* and James T. Farrell's *My Baseball Diary,* the first reprints in a new baseball series I was editing for our university press. I was also going to meet Eliot Asinof, who was driving up to Cooperstown to discuss his new novel and its publication in our series.

The fourth symposium became a confluence of baseball history for me, though I had no idea of how the more contemporary aspects of baseball were going to lure me once again into the darker side of Cooperstown. As an academic I gave what I thought was a responsible paper on the claims for Alfred H. Spink's neglected *America's National Game* as the first standard history of baseball instead of Albert G. Spalding's popular *Our National Game.* As a diehard Pirate fan, I delighted in the new Roberto Clemente exhibit in the Hall of Fame with its wonderful artifacts, including baseballs autographed by the 1960 and 1971 World Series champion Pittsburgh teams. As a lover of the game of baseball, I walked reverently along the Hall of Fame time line with Eliot Asinof as my guide, stood in front of the display for the 1919 Chicago White Sox, and listened to him talk about his difficulties in getting the surviving members of the team to talk about the Black Sox scandal for his book, *Eight Men Out,* because they were either angry or afraid.

What I didn't know was that another baseball celebrity, in Cooperstown to sign autographs at one of the baseball shops, was also to become my guide to the scandalous and sensational side of baseball and would lead me to my most shocking discovery. Clete Boyer, the third baseman on the championship New York Yankee teams of the early 1960s, seemed like a nice enough fellow when I met him at one of the local restaurants my first night in Cooperstown. He handled himself with the grace of a converted shortstop by reminding everyone that Brooks Robinson had played third base every time one of our overly worshipful symposiasts kept describing him as the greatest fielding third baseman in the history of baseball. He also responded politely, but without promising anything, to an invitation to attend a session at the symposium on baseball salaries and to play in the annual townball game. I doubted I'd ever see Clete Boyer again, unless I wanted to pay for his autograph, but I had no doubt in my mind which side he'd be on at the townball game if the Cooperstown Black Sox had something to do with it.

I had no idea how ubiquitous Clete Boyer was to become at my fourth symposium. He did show up at the session on baseball salaries, but I didn't get a chance to see him because my session was scheduled at the same time. Because of Boyer, my own session in the spacious National Pastime Gallery was so sparsely attended I yearned for the good old days in the Masonic Lodge and for the companionship of the billiard table. Afterwards, the hottest rumor circulating at the symposium was that Clete Boyer was coming to the townball game and had agreed to take a time at bat. My mind, however, was focused on pitching once again in the game and leading my team to victory against the corrupting forces that had undermined townball. If that meant throwing my blooper ball to Clete Boyer, well let's just see if he could do what Ted Williams did to Rip Sewell in the 1946 All-Star Game.

If I had the Baseball God–like power to write the script for the townball game, I would have conjured up another pitcher's duel between the thrower and me, given our team a one-tally lead, and had Clete Boyer pop out on my now legendary hesitation/blooper pitch to end the game. But none of that was to happen. The organizer of the townball game, not content this year with his interminable lecture and instructions, decided to be the thrower for both teams. When we lined up for sides, he also insisted that some of the more experienced players switch teams and even pulled a few of the infamous number twos, including my rival thrower of the past two years, onto my side. With Clete Boyer nowhere in sight and Eliot Asinof in attendance with my wife, we took the field, but, with only one or two ringers on our side, we still lost by over twenty tallies.

But this year's townball game had one defining, apparently redeeming moment for me. Clete Boyer finally showed up near the end of the game and did take a time at bat for the other side, as if they needed another ringer. He swung at the first pitch and, not surprisingly, lined the ball up the middle. Fortunately, the ball hit a large clump of grass and took a high hop right to me in my position behind the second stake. When I looked up, I saw Clete Boyer frozen between the home and first stake, apparently confused by all the yelling. I threw the ball across the pasture and, proving the baseball adage about being more lucky than good, soaked the ex-Yankee as he turned toward the first stake.

I remember running off the field and gloating to my wife and Eliot Asinof, an admitted Yankee fan, that no matter what happened at townball, I could now claim I was the one who soaked Clete Boyer. All the rest of it—the rigging of teams, the humiliating defeats—seemed incidental to my one shining moment on a Cooperstown cow pasture. After the game ended and we headed to the basement of the 1819 Inn for our postgame indoor picnic, I felt a kind of radical or restored innocence. Soaking Clete Boyer had purged my soul of the townball scandal and restored my faith in the redemptive power of baseball and the emotional magic of the Hall of Fame. I even felt like a bit of a celebrity when my wife and I, as Eliot Asinof's escorts, were invited to go through the buffet line first and sit at the table of honor.

Having taught literature for thirty years, I know that foolish pride precedes a tragic fall, so I should have seen what was coming. After we got our food, I offered to go up to the bar for a celebratory round of Old Slugger. When I got back, my seat beside my wife had been taken by the now ubiquitous Clete Boyer. My wife, who had spent the last thirty-five years of her life taking care of my needs and claimed she enjoyed the domestic side of marriage, took her eyes off Boyer long enough to tell me she thought "poor Mr. Boyer" was hungry, and would I mind going back up to the buffet for another plate of food and maybe bring another bottle of Old Slugger. A little later, when a coffee tray was brought around, my wife interrupted her rapt conversation with Boyer long enough to let me know that "Cletis" would probably like some coffee and would I bring her a cup as well.

It wasn't easy going from townball hero to hand servant to Clete Boyer and his new admirer. What made things even more difficult, however, was the realization that Boyer, who seemed to be oozing charm from every pore, had been teammates with Mickey Mantle,

Whitey Ford, and, worst of all, Jim Bouton, who had exposed the seamy side of ballplayers and their baseball groupies in the notorious *Ball Four.* Seated across the round table from Boyer and my wife, I couldn't hear what they were talking about, but my growing fear was that I was witness to the horrifying transformation of my Baseball Anita into a Baseball Annie. When my wife asked me to take a picture of the two of them, I remember telling Boyer that I knew he had good hands because of his reputation as a slick-fielding third baseman, so I'd like to see them on the table before I snapped the camera.

Despite my fears, my wife didn't run off with Clete Boyer that evening. They hugged at the end of the banquet, and, in a display of baseball gallantry, he kissed her hand in farewell. As good as I had felt running off the cow pasture after soaking Clete Boyer, my wife obviously felt much better after spending a few hours in the company of her Cletis. As we drove back to the inn, she seemed serenely contented with herself and, in contrast to my shameful gloating after the town-ball game, she seemed to be quietly glowing in the aftermath of her own triumph.

I was too crestfallen and my wife too radiant to press for details that night, but as we began our long ride home the next day I was given a full account of her evening with Clete Boyer. While I sat across from the two of them and, thanks to Jim Bouton, imagined the worst, Boyer was doing something to my wife that I hadn't done for a long time. He was paying tribute to her beauty. What she remembered was Boyer's gallantry—how he rose from his chair when she excused herself, how he held her chair on her return and, as she sat down, looked over at Eliot Asinof and said, "isn't she class?" She was impressed by Boyer's display of respect in the company of Asinof, by his honesty in talking about his personal life, and his generosity in responding to the symposiasts who came over to the table to pay their respects.

Of course, in the midst of painting Clete Boyer as knightly in conduct and herself as maidenly in response, she did describe a moment that hinted at *Ball Four* more than it suggested a baseball Tristram and Isolde. At one point, Boyer showed my wife his 1964 World Series Championship ring and told her he'd been offered ten thousand dollars for it. When she asked him what he was going to do, he said he was thinking about giving it to her. When I stupidly asked my wife what she would have done had her Cletis offered her the ring if she were willing to sleep with him, she casually and with a twinkle in her eye told me we probably could have used the money.

As we drove back to southern Illinois, I tried to put into perspective what I had learned about baseball after four trips to the Hall of Fame and wondered whether my psyche could survive another trip to Cooperstown. If I reduced my experiences to a moral fable, I might offer, among other things, the axiom that you should be careful rounding first base because you never know what or whom you are stepping on to get to second. If I wanted to turn my experiences into a history lesson, I might conclude that no matter where, when, or in what form you play the game, there's always someone, whether it's a symposium townballer or a professional owner or player, willing to bend the rules to win a game. Returning to home plate has an innocent appeal, but it's also the way you get ahead in the game; and if it takes getting ringers, or spending more money, or enhancing your performance with the latest miracle of science, well it's in the nature of the game and its history.

As for interpreting my wife's newfound love of baseball, I've tried to resist the traditional notion of baseball as the game of life, but it can, on occasion, shed a little light on human nature. I went to Cooperstown to rescue my soul from nearly a decade of Machiavellian politics, and my wife came along to make sure I didn't get lost—English professors have a notoriously poor sense of direction. While I yearned and searched for my boyhood innocence, my love of baseball ended up luring me into a knowledge of the complex and controversial nature of baseball history and the sometimes sad humanity of the game.

My wife, however, content to tolerate baseball for the sake of her marriage, discovered, thanks to an ex-Yankee and not her distracted husband, that charm, enchantment, and joy are still possible even in a Cooperstown cow pasture. As we drove home, I wondered if my tattered soul was ready for another plunge into baseball history at Cooperstown, but my radiant wife could hardly wait until next year.

◆ 2 ◆

The Word of Baseball:
Creating a Narrative

In W. P. Kinsella's *Shoeless Joe,* Eddie Scissons, an old fraud who claims to be the oldest living Chicago Cub, delivers a revivalist sermon from the bleachers to a small audience of baseball immortals, true believers, and even a baseball doubting Thomas or two. Scissons's message to those assembled is that the faithful need to preserve and speak the word of baseball: "'Have you the word of baseball living inside you? Has the word of baseball become a part of you? Do you live it, play it, digest it, forever? Let an old man tell you to make the word of baseball your life. Walk into the world and speak of baseball.'"

The apparent irony of this scene in a baseball novel rich in sentiment but notably lacking in ironic moments is that Eddie Scissons delivers his sermon just before his death and just after the humiliating exposure of his great lie: that he pitched for the 1908–10 Chicago Cubs. Yet, while Eddie's lie appears to undermine the message of the sermon, his love of baseball and his faith in the word redeem his own fallen spirit. Though his punishment for falsely claiming a place for himself among baseball's legendary heroes has been to watch "Kid" Scissons, his dream self, relieve Cub legend Third Finger Brown and fail to get anyone out, Eddie still wins his place among baseball immortals because he believes in the word of baseball: "'It takes more than an infinite ERA to shake my faith.'"

Though humiliated in life and seemingly defeated by death, Eddie Scissons reaches his dream because he lived with the word of baseball inside him and made the word of baseball his life. Eddie's confirmation into baseball immortality comes about when Joe Jackson asks that his teammates be a part of Eddie's funeral. As the players, Eddie's beloved "baseball boys," file past the coffin, Ray Kinsella, the novel's narrator and master builder of the field of dreams where Eddie Scissons will now be buried, gazes at his handiwork and feels that if he were to look again in *The Baseball Encyclopedia,* he would now find an entry for Edward "Kid" Scissons: "And under that would be the details of Eddie's three seasons as a relief pitcher with the Cubs: his won-and-lost record, number of innings pitched, ERA, strikeouts, bases on balls, and batting record. I have the feeling. I have the feeling."

Eddie Scissons's undying faith in the word of baseball and Ray Kinsella's heartfelt vision of the transformative power of the word are fundamental to baseball's narrative tradition. From preeminent pioneer Henry Chadwick, elected to the Hall of Fame in 1938, to recent Spink Award recipient Joseph Durso, baseball's writers have spread the word of baseball by glorifying the game and mythologizing its players. In narratives ranging from journalistic essays and oral histories to biographies, histories, and baseball fiction, writers have generated an entire mythology of baseball, replete with a myth of origin, a fabled past, and a pantheon of baseball immortals. By envisioning baseball as the stuff of dreams, these narratives have transmuted the game from a pastoral event into a spring ritual and cultural icon. They have also fostered a national faith in baseball as America's game by closely associating the playing of the game with the aspirations of a democratic society and the fulfillment of the American Dream.

It may be, as A. G. Spalding once claimed, that baseball begins with a boy tossing a ball into the air, but the words of baseball's faithful have transfigured Spalding's youth into an archetype of rugged and determined individualism and exalted the flight of the ball as a soaring metaphor of connectedness and continuity for generations of Americans. The poet Donald Hall, for example, a true believer in the word of baseball, takes Spalding's simple image of a boy tossing a ball to another boy and transforms it into a profound game of catch between fathers and sons: "Baseball is the generations, looping backward forever with a million apparitions of sticks and balls, cricket and rounders, and the games the Iroquois played in Connecticut before the English came. Baseball is fathers and sons playing catch, lazy and murderous, wild and controlled, the profound archaic song of birth, growth, age, and death. This diamond encloses what we are."

W. P. Kinsella extends Donald Hall's vision of generations of fathers playing catch with sons by taking his fictional fathers and sons into the realm of the magical, miraculous, and supernatural. In *Shoeless Joe* the faith and love of the living son not only recovers and completes the dead father's unfulfilled dream of playing major-league baseball, it eases the pain of self-exiled J. D. Salinger by fulfilling his lost boyhood dream of trying out for the 1938 New York Giants of Mel Ott and Carl Hubbell. In Kinsella's *The Iowa Baseball Confederacy*, the narrator, Gideon Clarke, slips through a crack in time to recover his father's lost dream of a Fourth of July exhibition game between the 1908 world-champion Chicago Cubs and the Iowa Baseball Confederacy all-star team, only to encounter and eventually play in a game that refuses to end until an act of love allows the narrator to return from the field of a dream-turned-nightmare to the land of the living. Filled with some of the most outlandish characters and bizarre events to appear in a Kinsella narrative, *The Iowa Baseball Confederacy* plays out a seemingly boundless game in a biblical downpour, while Theodore Roosevelt pops in to praise the courage and devotion of the players and take a time at bat (he strikes out), and Leonardo da Vinci floats by in a hot-air balloon to watch a few innings of the game he invented: "Who else could come up with such perfect dimensions?"

The dream narratives of Hall and Kinsella, if taken together, envision baseball as generative and cyclical, yet somehow transcendent and transformative as well. They also validate baseball historian Warren Goldstein's claim that baseball's narrative tradition is grounded in powerful emotions, that the "emotional energy of most good baseball writing is generational," and that the nature of the game itself, because of the gaps between batters and innings, encourages "dreaming and dreaminess." For another true believer, A. Bartlett Giamatti, this dreaminess corresponds to no less than the primitive and recurrent need in the human mind "to think that something lasts forever." Baseball's green fields and its seasonal play appeal to the instinctual yearning for a "state of being" resistant to mutability and decay, even if the game itself is really "meant to stop." When it does, it betrays "precisely what it promised": "It breaks your heart. It is designed to break your heart. The game begins in the spring, when everything begins again, and it blossoms in the summer, filling the afternoons and evenings, and then as soon as the chill rains come, it stops and leaves you to face the fall alone. You count on it, rely on it to buffer the passage of time, to keep the memory of sunshine and high skies alive, and then just when the days are all twilight, when you need it the most, it stops."

Giamatti's celebrated evocation of baseball's compelling and heartbreaking grip on those in search of a field for dreams of promise and renewal is certainly consistent with Hall's paean to generations of fathers playing catch with sons and Kinsella's magical narrations of sons rebuilding or replaying the lost dreams of their fathers. Yet the same generational emotions and powerful faith in dreams are often at the heart of baseball narratives that otherwise appear as social documents or historical reconstructions. In his preface to the enlarged edition of *The Glory of Their Times*, Lawrence Ritter writes that he first thought his "strange crusade" of interviewing old ballplayers "had been inspired by the death of Ty Cobb in 1961" and that he was pursuing "a social goal, recording for posterity the remembrance of a sport that had played such a significant role in American life in the early years of the twentieth century." Years later, however, he realized his journey was more personal than social because his father died about the same time as Ty Cobb: "Still vivid in my memory is the day, when I was nine years old, that my father took me by the hand to my first big-league baseball game. It seems to me now that I was trying to recapture that unforgettable ritual of childhood and draw closer to a father I would never see again—and I think that, through *The Glory of Their Times,* I somehow succeeded."

Just as Lawrence Ritter places his interviews with old-time players within the emotional context of attending his first major-league game with his father, Roger Kahn, in *The Boys of Summer,* frames his narrative of the passing of the golden era of the Brooklyn Dodgers within his emotional relationship with his father. Before Kahn even begins his story of the boys of summer at their play and in their ruin, he writes about his early childhood and how "the bond between my father and me was baseball." Preparatory to his account of the Dodger glory years of Robinson, Snider, Reese, and Campanella, he remembers the way the 1941 Dodger pennant-winning season of Dolf Camilli and Whitlow Wyatt stirred his father's memory of Zack Wheat and the 1920 Dodger pennant and allowed father and son to share the same excitement and emotion, if not the same team: "for the first time we were men together." And when death disrupts the ceremonies of innocence between father and son, Kahn's narrative shifts its perspective from the passing glory of great baseball players and teams to the greater tragedy of the passing of baseball-loving and baseball-playing men: "The team was broken up and with my father dead there was no one with whom I wanted to consider that tragedy, and because there was no one I recognized that the breaking of a team was not like greater tragedy: incompleteness, unspoken words, unmade music, withheld love, the failure ever to sum up or say good-bye."

While *The Glory of Their Times* and *The Boys of Summer* are re-

markable in their social and historical record of fading generations of
ballplayers, the emotional wellspring for each work lies in what Kahn,
in writing about Dodger fathers and their sons, describes as "father
and son circling one another in a spiky maze of love." Baseball's narratives, however, whether histories or oral histories, fictions or biographies, have a way of connecting and drawing fathers and sons together, tapping into the emotions of their relationships in spite of the
confusing maze of generational gaps and conflicts. Through the lyrical evocation or pure memory of a son playing catch with his father,
or the generational ritual of a father taking his son to his first major-
league baseball game, or the intimate experience of father and son
sharing in the memories and excitement of past and present seasons,
baseball's writers often evoke a dream narrative in which fathers and
sons, the past and the present, the remembered and the imagined, are
joined in a celebration of baseball as enduring and unalterable.

In his essay "The Interior Stadium," Roger Angell accounts for this
dream narrative by claiming that baseball, for the faithful, is never
merely a return to or a restoration of things past. Because of the game's
leisurely pace and its seasonal play, it invites reflection, discovery, and
invention. And for the truly thoughtful and caring, baseball eventually yields the magic of its appeal as a generational and national game.
It brings generations and a people together because of "its vividness—
the absolutely distinct inner vision we retain of that hitter, that eager
base runner, of however long ago." This inner vision is further enhanced by the unpredictability and surprise within the patterns and
rituals of games and seasons and the wondrous ability of baseball's
great players to transcend form and chance and transform the game
itself into an image of their greatness. For Angell, these qualities—the
game's vividness and intensity, its unpredictability and surprise, and
its transcendent and transformative plays and performers—engender
baseball's most defining and compelling characteristic: its sense of timelessness. Baseball remains rustic, innocent, and dreamy for the true
believer because baseball's field of play appears "seamless and invisi-

ble, a bubble within which players move at exactly the same pace and rhythms as all their predecessors. This is the way the game was played in our youth and in our fathers' youth, and even back then—back in the country days—there must have been the same feeling that time could be stopped."

Roger Angell's emotionally charged vision of baseball's eternal youthfulness merely reflects the most commonly held view and the most widely claimed attribute of the traditional baseball narrative. Whether baseball is imagined as the green fuse that ignites the passion and hope of the baseball faithful each spring, or the Ariadne thread of memory and revery that leads biographers and historians from the uncertain present to the dreamy past, or the emotional halo that envelops generations of fathers and sons, the traditional role of baseball narratives is to affirm the essential nature of the game as timeless, boundless, and changeless, at least in its promise.

This visionary faith in the power of baseball to transcend the confinements of time and space and defy the physical conditions of mutability and decay is clearly essential to writers who use the word of baseball to imagine magical fields of dreams or evoke green fields or invisible stadia of the mind. The same holds true for writers who envision generations of fathers playing catch with sons or honor the boys of past summers at their play. This faith in baseball's capacity to restore the most deeply felt emotions of our youth and evoke the most profound dream of the human spirit even finds its way into the narratives of baseball's most skeptical and cynical writers, those who use the words of baseball to comment on the historical or cultural significance of the game but resist and sometimes mock the claims for baseball's dreaminess.

Among the most persistent of baseball's doubting Thomases, Stephen Jay Gould has been highly critical of writers who dream too much into baseball. In "The Creation Myths of Cooperstown," Gould sees the romanticizing of baseball as silly and the mythologizing of its players and history as so much "'bullbleep.'" In the same essay, he also claims that the "silliest and most tendentious of baseball writing tries to wrest profundity from the spectacle of grown men hitting a ball with a stick." Yet Gould's criticism of baseball's dream-makers belies his own romantic tendencies in other baseball essays to evoke sweet memories of childhood or create moments of pure hero worship. He follows his discussion of the extinction of the .400 hitter, for example, with a postscript that qualifies his scientific data by recalling and celebrating Don Larsen's perfect game in the 1956 World Series, framed within Gould's own childhood memory of the event, as a tribute to baseball's "eternal possibility of transcendence." "The Streak of Streaks," Gould's essay on another transcendent event, Joe DiMaggio's fifty-six game hitting streak, not only evokes memories of fathers and sons but one of the most tendentious and transcendental claims made by any baseball narrative written about one of the game's legendary heroes: "DiMaggio activated the greatest and most unattainable dream of all humanity, the hope and chimera of all sages and shamans: he cheated death at least for a while."

Even in the postmodern world of kiss-and-tell biographies and autobiographies, revisionist histories, and deconstructive fictions, baseball's writers have kept their faith in the dream narrative and its evocation of eternal youthfulness even as they question baseball's traditional values, debunk the game's legends, and expose the moral mistakes responsible for baseball's decline as the national pastime. A catalyst for the development of a more cynical postmodern baseball narrative, Jim Bouton's *Ball Four* is widely accepted and praised as unique and revolutionary for its time in its criticism and rejection of baseball's "indiscriminate hero-making." Yet while Bouton attacks Organized Baseball's stupidity, pettiness, and hypocrisy, he preserves, as a ballplayer, his boyhood love of the game and his dreams of glory on the playing field: "I dream all these things. I really do. So there's no use asking me why I'm here, why a reasonably intelligent thirty-year-old man who has lost his fastball is still struggling to play baseball, holding on—literally— with his fingertips. The dreams are the answer."

Bouton's faith in baseball's dream narrative of eternal youthfulness and his own dreams of fame and immortality are his answer to the question of how the game of baseball keeps its hold on someone who has spent a good piece of his life gripping a baseball. The answer to the question of how baseball keeps the same hold on someone who spent a good piece of his life gripping a bat appears in Ted Williams's autobiographical *My Turn at Bat,* published in 1969, the same year as Bouton's misbegotten season in *Ball Four.* In an outspoken and sometimes bitter narrative, Williams claims that, unlike players who refuse to let go of the dream, he is glad his career is over and "wouldn't want to go back." As for baseball's dream narrative and its lure of eternal youthfulness, Williams flatly states: "I certainly do not have a youth wish." Yet, even as he dismisses his relationship with his father and rails against baseball writers, the custodians of the word of baseball, Williams readily admits to a childhood dream of becoming the greatest hitter who ever lived: "If there was ever a man born to be a hitter, it was me. As a kid, I wished it on every falling star." As for the larger dream, on the occasion of his induction into the Hall of Fame Williams proclaimed baseball as the embodiment of the American Dream—"Baseball gives every American boy a chance to excel"—and his induction as the fulfillment of his own boyhood dreams—"how much I wanted it. Just a boy and his dreams."

Baseball's powerful grip on the emotional life of its players emerges again and again from baseball's narratives, especially from autobiographical accounts of baseball from the inside. At the end of *The Long Season,* a book praised by baseball novelist Mark Harris and others for its truthfulness and lack of sentiment, Jim Brosnan describes the heightened emotional state of ballplayers at season's end and the dreamy lure of next season: "On the last day of the season baseball is a game that professionals really do *play;* it no longer seems like work to them. It is virtually impossible for a player to convince himself that he will never play the game again. On the last day of the season baseball, truly, is in the blood." While Brosnan's book, in its determination to reveal the inside story of baseball, anticipates Bouton's more outrageous and outspoken narrative in *Ball Four,* its conclusion explains why a used-up, thirty-year-old pitcher like Bouton, with nothing left to his career but a trick pitch and a reputation as a clubhouse lawyer, would struggle to play yet one more season of major-league baseball. Brosnan's conclusion also explains why ballplayers, even a bitter Ted Williams or a vindictive Ty Cobb, tend to relive their careers within narratives of youthful dreams and dreamy memories of a golden age: "Every baseball season is just long enough for each player to do something to which he can look back with satisfaction. On the last days of the season those are the moments that you want to remember, and probably those are the memories that make you a little sad."

From *The Glory of Their Times* and Donald Honig's *Baseball When the Grass Was Real* to Danny Peary's *We Played the Game* and Larry Moffi's *This Side of Cooperstown,* oral histories have collected these treasured memories of major-league ballplayers who, in Lawrence Ritter's words, believe they "chased a dream, and, at least for a time, caught up with it and lived it." Like baseball's autobiographical writing and its traditional evocation of youthful dreams and perfect moments, oral histories have often forged gold mosaics out of the reveries of old-time ballplayers. Often envisioning themselves as participants in a legendary past, these ballplayers have had a tendency to transform the physical hardships of their careers into the emotional thrill of playing baseball and an abiding love for the game. Rube Marquard's dreamy recollection in *The Glory of Their Times* that "every single day of all the years I spent in the Big Leagues was a thrill for me . . . a dream come true" and Chief Meyer's romantic claim that he and his contemporaries played "just for the love of [baseball] . . . and would have paid *them* just to let us play" have become mere commonplaces in the tradition of baseball's oral histories.

Even baseball histories, unless moments of scandal and disgrace decree a darker vision, have added their own measures to baseball's dream narrative. From A. G. Spalding's *America's National Game* to

John Helyar's *Lords of the Realm,* these histories often portray players as heroes and demigods and parade them through narratives that routinely use elements of legend, fable, and myth to tell their stories. Standard baseball histories, like the multivolume works of David Quentin Voigt and Harold Seymour, include sections on golden and silver ages and chapters on the making of heroes and the heroic baseball life. Voigt's *American Baseball* consistently identifies baseball's most prosperous and dynamic eras with the rise and eventual deification of baseball heroes ranging from Cap Anson and Babe Ruth to Joe DiMaggio and Reggie Jackson. Seymour, echoing Joseph Campbell's study of the mythical hero of a thousand faces, claims that this "idolization of ball players lies in man's urge to create heroes. . . . For some people ball players satisfy this need because in ball players they see living evidence that certain values and assumptions deep in the American psyche still have validity."

In *Baseball and the American Dream,* its title a dead giveaway of the book's historical perspective, Joseph Durso validates Seymour's comments on baseball and the American psyche by claiming that his narrative "is not exactly a history of baseball" but more "a story" of a game that, in the midst of change, "stays 'the national pastime' . . . it plays out the tradition of 'the American dream' in public view for all the world to see and share—in Tennyson's words: to strive, to seek, to find, and not to yield." Durso's appropriation of the concluding lines of Tennyson's "Ulysses" to celebrate baseball's enduring and unalterable character is perfectly fitting for baseball's traditional narrative. Just as Tennyson's poem pays homage to a defiant and still heroic Ulysses who refuses to surrender to old age and death and sails forth once again into the fabulous and mythical realm of adventure, baseball's traditional narrative elevates and honors a game capable of defying time and evoking in the true believer a vision of eternal youthfulness and heroic adventure.

Baseball's traditional narrative, consistent in form but kaleidoscopic in expression, is an old man urging the faithful to preserve and speak the word of baseball or a young man building a baseball heaven for his dead father; it is also a middle-aged poet imagining generations of fathers playing catch with sons or a dying commissioner cultivating green fields of the mind. Baseball's dream narrative is capable of gripping the intelligence and imagination of a skeptical paleontologist or a cynical ballplayer; and it can give a youthful voice to an old-time ballplayer or mythical wings to a baseball historian. Above all, for baseball's writers, it has been the perfect expression, at least within the context of American history and culture, of the irresistible lure of dreaminess and the emotional and imaginative need to believe in that which we dream. Once touched by the dream, baseball's writers have taken Eddie Scissons at his word, spreading the narratives of baseball either to define a nation's aspirations and character, or to reconnect the emotional relationship between the generations, or simply to rediscover, in the fading memories of times past, the lost dream of youthfulness or the lost youth of the dreamer.

◆ 3 ◆

This Must Be Heaven: Baseball's Paradise Lost and Regained

In W. P. Kinsella's *Shoeless Joe*, when a redeemed Joe Jackson emerges out of an Iowa cornfield to play left field on the perfectly constructed and cultivated outfield prepared for him by Ray Kinsella, he looks up at his loving and devoted savior and declares, "'This must be heaven,'" only to be told, "'No. It's Iowa.'" Moments later, Ray Kinsella, after gazing upon the miracle of his creation, has second thoughts and whispers to himself, "'I think you're right, Joe.'"

Occasionally, less miraculous baseball narratives appear to slip out of the mythical aura and heroic trappings of baseball tradition either because a player has irrevocably lost his dream or the historical moment or event is too real and painful to be modified or transformed even by baseball's dreaminess. Refraining from the use of magical realism to convert human failure into supernatural heroics or ugly scandal into misguided innocence and good-heartedness, these narratives have tried to gain an undistorted view and a clearer understanding of baseball either by looking inside the dream or by finding some outside perspective from which to judge the dream itself. While some of the narratives have found a hell lurking beneath baseball's heaven, others have found the dream still alive in the most unlikely places and hopeless situations or have tried to replace the undistilled dream of baseball with a moral or aesthetic vision of baseball's playing field and its men at work.

Pat Jordan's *A False Spring,* for example, is a brutally honest, at times even devastating, account of a young pitcher's complete failure to live up to his phenomenal talent and the dream of "no-hitters and World Series triumphs" concocted for him out of his older brother's expectations. Rather than trying to relive or recapture the dream through the word of baseball, Jordan's narrative simply tries to see his failure not within the scaffolding of youthful dreams and baseball mythology but as the outcome of his emotional immaturity and his unwillingness to accept the responsibility for losing control of his fastball and his personal conduct. Rather than offering up a paean to eternal youthfulness even as the dreamer is defeated by his own sad humanity, *A False Spring* unveils a baseball world whose mythology stunts emotional growth by creating the false perception that a player's life will never change as long as he holds on to his boyhood dreams. Rather than glorifying baseball, *A False Spring* becomes Pat Jordan's struggle, ten years after the end of his career, to come to terms with the profound and, in Jordan's case, harmful influence of the dream of baseball on the shape and substance of his life: "I still think of myself not as a writer who once pitched, but as a pitcher who happens to be writing just now."

No such emotional confusion exists, however, for Roger Kahn in *Good Enough to Dream,* the narrative account of Kahn's year as the president of the Class A minor-league Utica Blue Sox. As the title indicates, Kahn's narrative never questions the dream of baseball. It opens with an evocation to the youthful hope of playing major-league baseball and the ritual companionship between baseball-loving fathers and sons. It also follows a pennant race that ends the way pennant races are meant to end in dream narratives, with the narrator's team eventually winning the league championship. Even with its traditional scaffolding, however, *Good Enough to Dream* narrates a season in which a writer, whose own hope of playing major-league baseball expired at the age of nine, becomes part of the collective personality of an independently operated but nearly bankrupt minor-league team whose cast of misfits and rejects turns out to be good enough at season's end to become champions even as their careers and their dreams fade out.

For Pat Jordan, writing about his misbegotten baseball career gives him a perspective on the loneliness and betrayal hidden within baseball's traditional dream of eternal youthfulness and ageless triumphs. For Roger Kahn, writing about his year as president of the Utica Blue Sox gives him the chance to recover the dream from the most dismal and desperate of baseball worlds, where, at its best, the game is played out in the fading and discordant notes of a minor key. While Pat Jordan finds the promise of a glorious life in baseball betrayed by the false dream of throwing the perfect pitch, Roger Kahn, resisting the narrative "interplay of ancient gods and modern baseball," discovers the living dream among far-less-than-heroic players who have fun playing baseball and even a passion for doing well no matter what the limits of their talent and destiny. The advice Roger Kahn once was given about becoming a writer also seems appropriate for those who play the game of baseball, especially for those who find a hard reality instead of the dream: "You had better like writing if you intend to be a writer."

While Jordan's autobiographical narrative uncovers the fear and loathing often obscured by the word of baseball, Kahn's story of the Utica Blue Sox finds the dream of baseball still alive among baseball's most forlorn outcasts. In Eliot Asinof's *Eight Men Out,* the narrative includes both Jordan's revelation of the dream corrupted and Kahn's understanding of the source of the game's real passion. As a baseball chronicle, Asinof's narrative of the fixing of the 1919 World Series serves as a witness to the terrible fall from grace of one of baseball's greatest teams: "There was a growing mythology about this great team;

the public had placed a stamp of invincibility on it." As a baseball story, it brings to life the dramatic moment in baseball history in which the actions of a handful of baseball's legendary heroes betrayed the public's trust in the game and corrupted baseball's youthful dream. Stephen Jay Gould, his "bullbleep" detector as ubiquitous in baseball narratives as Captain Ahab's white whale in *Moby Dick,* goes so far as to claim in his introduction to *Eight Men Out* that the Black Sox scandal changed the character, history, and mythology of baseball by "dispelling forever the cardinal legend of innocence. Innocence is precious, but truth is better."

To get to the truth, Asinof's narrative becomes a journey into baseball's heart of darkness: its close association from its earliest days with gamblers and the persistent rumors and stories throughout its history about players throwing games. Within this narrative context the fixing of the 1919 World Series, as Gould contends, was clearly more than a passing crisis for the game of baseball or a momentary setback for baseball's dream makers. It now becomes the historical moment, because of the significance of the World Series to American culture, when baseball finally revealed its darkest secret and its hidden shame to a shocked and disbelieving American public.

Once this horrible truth is recognized and understood, Asinof's narrative, to recover its own balance and render a proper judgment of baseball's greatest scandal, assumes a moral voice and viewpoint appropriate to the betrayal of the public's faith and confidence in the word and the dream of baseball at the time of the 1919 World Series: "The year before, America had won the war in the image of nobility and humanity. 'Saving Europe from the Hun' was a sacrificial act. Our pride in victory was the essence of American pride itself. Baseball was the manifestation of the greatest of America at play. It was our national game; its stars were national heroes, revered by kids and adults alike, in all classes of society. In the public mind, the image was pure and patriotic."

The problem in *Eight Men Out,* once Asinof turns to a moral perspective, is that his narrative of the Black Sox scandal, while rejecting baseball's mythological scaffolding, takes on the simplistic trappings of a moral romance with its ready cast of heroes, villains, and victims. In the moral universe of *Eight Men Out,* those who have the courage to expose the fixing of the World Series, like reporter Hugh Fullerton, are the narrative's heroes. Those responsible for the corrupting circumstances that invited scandal into the game of baseball, like the greedy and tyrannical Charles Comiskey, owner of the Chicago White Sox, and the notorious Arnold Rothstein, the gangster who provided the money for the fix, are clearly the narrative's villains. The American public and by extension the public's dream of baseball as pure and patriotic become the obvious victims.

As for the players, the eight conspirators now banned forever from baseball, a few notables escape the narrative's moral imperative and are forgiven, at least in *Eight Men Out,* because they retained, in spite of their grievous act against the integrity of baseball, an essential core of goodness and innocence. Accordingly, Buck Weaver, because of his great passion for the game and his persistent attempts to clear his name and return to baseball, becomes a sympathetic figure; and Joe Jackson, because of his great natural ability and his country innocence, while, like Weaver, never pardoned by baseball, is forgiven his sin and redeemed, at least in Asinof's narrative, by a closing tribute that transforms Jackson's ignorance of character into a tragic nobility: "To the local folk, he remained a hero, well liked and highly respected. He was never without their support, and the dignity of his talent never seemed to dwindle."

Asinof's moral vision of the 1919 World Series scandal and his qualified judgment of the Black Sox players is typical of baseball narratives about historical events or periods that threaten the public's faith in baseball as the stuff of dreams and legends. These narratives, while highly critical and judgmental in perspective, often create a black-and-white universe populated by romantic or rebellious heroes and demonized or tyrannical villains. At times they even embellish their moral romances or romantic tragedies with the satanic or apocalyptic to dramatize the disruption and chaos inherent in a disillusioned and troubled baseball world.

Mike Sowell's *The Pitch That Killed,* a historical account of the fatal beaning of Ray Chapman by Carl Mays, uses a narrative strategy similar to Asinof's in dramatizing baseball's most horrifying moment on the playing field. In Sowell's romantic tragedy the belligerent, hated Carl Mays is rendered in sharp contrast to the smiling, beloved Ray Chapman. Chapman is presented as the model ballplayer, handsome and flawless in bearing and conduct, idolized by family, teammates, and fans, the perfect symbol of baseball's eternal youthfulness. Mays, with his evil reputation as a beanball pitcher, his freakish submarine delivery, and his alienation from even his own teammates, is portrayed and judged as an unrepentant and unredeemed blackguard. While Chapman is immortalized in Sowell's narrative as baseball's hero dying young and even reincarnated in Joe Sewell's pennant-winning performance after Chapman's death, Mays is frozen and damned forever in baseball history as a sinister figure, responsible for major-league baseball's only fatality, associated at career's end with rumors of fixing the 1921 World Series, and blackballed from the Hall of Fame. Sowell's *The Pitch That Killed* virtually assures the memory of Carl Mays as one of baseball's arch villains: "To the end, he never was able to escape that pitch."

The acclaim from baseball's faithful for conventional moral romances and romantic tragedies masquerading as revisionist histories and biographies suggests that baseball's narratives on occasion fulfill some emergent need to expose and purge the barbarians, villains, and demons willing to betray the word of baseball and defile the dream. This need is especially acute in narratives that focus on some historical juncture, rupture, or action that contradicts or threatens the traditional view of baseball as timeless and perfect. These narratives, while forced to look at baseball through a glass darkly, have brought a moral perspective to baseball's dubious passage through moments and periods of greed, scandal, and violence and found that the fault lies not in the word or dream but in the conduct or action of some autocratic, self-serving owner or in some sociopathic, vengeful, or deluded ballplayer. The shocking, outrageous, and shameful in baseball's narratives often serve as moral signposts or object lessons warning the faithful that the only way of saving baseball from its own demons and madness is to find some way back to the saving grace of the game itself. The moral imperative of baseball's narrative romances and tragedies, even when confronted by gothic horrors, is to heed Eddie Scissons's sermon: to keep faith in the word of baseball and the purity of the game even when those most responsible for preserving baseball's dreamscape seem hell-bent on destroying it.

For some of baseball's writers, however, the polar vision of baseball as a heaven of faithful sons playing catch with redeemed fathers or a hell of diabolic owners and demented players casting dice for ownership of the game seems too extreme even for narratives easily given to mythological scaffolding, romantic trappings, and moral imperatives. Writers uncomfortable with baseball narratives that either sanctify or demonize sometimes look for a middle ground, some place or position between paradise and pandemonium where they can still find virtue and value in baseball without anointing the game with emotional halos or cleansing its history with romantic tragedies or moral purgatives. For some baseball narratives this middle ground lies in the craftsmanship and artistry of playing baseball. Instead of creating dreamy visions of legendary heroes performing on seamless and timeless fields of play or evoking hellish nightmares of diabolic villains jeopardizing the purity and perfection of the national pastime, narratives on the craft of baseball look at actual fields of play and real performances. Though less inclined to imagine baseball demigods and demons performing miraculous or horrific feats, these narratives still see the possibility of greatness and even perfection, but only in a responsibility to the game and a commitment to craft that raises the level of play to artistry.

This shift in perspective, emphasis, and appeal is clearly evident in Leonard Koppett's *A Thinking Man's Guide to Baseball,* a baseball narrative widely praised for its acknowledgment of the intelligence of the baseball fan, its understanding of the techniques of the game, and its appreciation of the hard work and dedication of the major-league player. Writing as "a daily baseball writer," Koppett assumes that the serious fan "would enjoy knowing more about Baseball" than what is available in reporting and broadcasting; that he or she would prefer baseball's truths to its "myths and clichés"; that he or she has "some curiosity" about baseball techniques as well as personalities; and that, as knowledgeable as a fan may be, there are certain aspects of baseball "that haven't come to your attention." For Koppett, these aspects have to do with baseball's realities, its "interaction, human fallibility, and unpredictability, and above all dynamics," and its artistry, the "intuitive and purposeful manipulation" of the strategies and forms of the game by players and managers for a "special result," the achievement of success and greatness on the field.

In *Men at Work,* George Will elevates Koppett's appeal to the serious fan by claiming that baseball is a sport for a literary culture. To enjoy the orderly and sequential nature of the game, "you have to be able to read it. Baseball requires baseball literacy." Instead of writing about baseball as the stuff of romance, even though baseball "is an activity to be loved," Will looks at baseball as work and argues that his narrative is an antiromantic exercise in the appreciation rather than the worship of those who appear heroic, but only because they care about their craft and have the determination to do well in their vocation. Rather than falling back on moral imperatives, Will finds the ethical within baseball's ability to teach "a general truth about excellence" and concludes that, instead of being compromised or threatened by change, the game actually benefits from change and gets better because of the intelligence and adaptability of baseball's most caring and dedicated performers.

Will's narrative strategy in *Men at Work* is to reveal this intelligence, adaptability, and dedication from different baseball perspectives—the manager; the pitcher; the batter; the defense—a strategy used even more extensively by Koppett in *A Thinking Man's Guide to Baseball*. While neither narrative completely escapes the lure of mythology and legend or the dramatics of moral romance and romantic tragedy, both emphasize the importance of getting to the truth by giving the reader the opportunity to see baseball as clearly and as comprehensively as possible. For Koppett and Will, if the writer, no matter what the private or public dream, can construct a perspective or even a series of perspectives for the observation of the game's realities, then the reader, provided with an unclouded view of baseball, can eventually discover baseball's truths and even learn to appreciate the beauty of the game itself.

Among the best examples of a balanced perspective in the often romanticized and moralized narratives of baseball lives are the bad-boy biographies written by Charles Alexander. Instead of reveling in the demonic, Alexander's biographies of Ty Cobb and Rogers Hornsby offer a carefully measured view of baseball's greatest player and its greatest right-handed hitter. Rather than exaggerating their personality flaws as manifestations of the psychotic mind at work on the baseball field, Alexander sees their obsessiveness and alienation as a reflection of their drive for perfection and their single-minded devotion to baseball. Alexander's Cobb was "the most volatile, the most fear-inspiring presence ever to appear on a baseball field," but he also had baseball's "most fiercely competitive spirit." As for the ill-tempered, brutally tactless, and "extraordinarily narrow-minded" Hornsby, Alexander claims that "he cared for little besides baseball." Perhaps baseball's most extreme examples and expressions of men at work, both Cobb and Hornsby so lived the word of baseball that they achieved greatness and immortality on the playing field because, according to Alexander, they cared for little else in life.

Among baseball's prolific commentators, perhaps Tom Boswell best illustrates the way a writer can balance his own view of baseball by looking at the game from as many positions or perspectives as possible. Boswell's writing fits so comfortably within baseball's traditional narrative that the titles of some of his essays—"How Life Imitates the World Series" and "Why Time Begins on Opening Day"—have become catch phrases in baseball's narrative tradition. His essay "The Fourth Dimension: Baseball and Memory," with its heartfelt celebration of "baseball's passion for the past," is the perfect complement to the green fields and invisible stadia of the mind evoked by A. Bartlett Giamatti and Roger Angell: "Because baseball is the mind game, it also is the memory game." Boswell is also capable of taking full advantage of the tendency of baseball's traditional narrative to cloak a player's betrayal of his own greatness and his subsequent fall from grace within the simple didactics of the moral romance or the heightened dramatics of the romantic tragedy. His commentary on Pete Rose, collected in *Cracking the Show,* portrays Rose as a self-made hero, the stuff of Horatio Alger romances, who fell victim to the larger-than-life adulation that transformed him into a baseball immortal: "If Rose is not a modern approximation of a tragic figure in Greek drama, then who would be?"

While Boswell admits that getting a perspective on Pete Rose is "especially difficult" and proves his point by describing Rose's banishment as a "righteous lynching," the strength of his commentaries lies in his ability to balance baseball's dreaminess and its realities by finding various perspectives on the game. In "Ballpark Wanderer," for example, he begins by claiming that major-league parks are "persistently and confidently unique" and that "each major league park has one best place to perch." In "This Ain't a Football Game. We Do This Every Day," Boswell sees baseball itself as a human kaleidoscope: "Each time we return to the game and its folk we see a different scene, a different mood, a different trait of character or twist of personality." In the same essay he goes so far as to suggest that baseball's greatest value is its contribution to America's mental health, its cultivation of a balanced temperament—"The sense of elemental sanity and order that we sometimes feel around baseball is not entirely a romantic wish; the game has at its core, a distinct therapeutic quality."

Whether romantic or therapeutic, Boswell's essays, ranging in topics from the delightful quirkiness of baseball board games and the old-fashioned charm of the College World Series to the intense drama of the World Series and the keen anticipation of opening day, have corroborated the broadest claims of baseball's narrative tradition while utilizing its rich and varied perspectives. They also confirm that for baseball's writers, from Henry Chadwick, who invented the box score and wrote the first official rule and guide books, to Thomas Boswell, who claims he is merely carrying on baseball's "rich verbal tradition," baseball has been and continues to be "the writer's game."

As the writer's game, baseball has been transformed by the words of novelists, historians, biographers, and journalists into narratives of magical dreams, moral romances, romantic tragedies, and aesthetic delights. These narratives in turn have invested baseball with visions of infinite possibilities and eternal youthfulness, perceived its significant and dramatic historical moments as tests of a nation's moral character, judged its players' fall from grace as tragic or apocalyptic, and elevated the strategies and playing of the game to the level of art. Baseball's writers have praised and kept faith in the word of baseball by developing a narrative tradition in the midst of social, political, and cultural change that is capable of evoking images of baseball as timeless, seamless, and self-delighting as well as instructive, cathartic, and purposeful. This narrative tradition, no matter how it expresses itself in form and content, has embodied the passionate need to dream our youthful dreams and to hope for the moment, like that awaiting J. D. Salinger in *Shoeless Joe*, in which we touch the dream: "'But what a story it will make . . . a man being able to touch the perfect dream. I'll write of it. I promise.'" For those who have written about baseball as the perfect dream, the narrative journey is emotional, ritual, and generational. In the dream narrative of Doris Kearns Goodwin, it begins with a father taking his daughter to her first major-league

game at Ebbets Field and culminates in a mother taking her three sons
to Fenway Park on a warm summer's day:

> If I close my eyes against the sun, all at once I'm back at Ebbets Field, a
> young girl once more in the presence of my father, watching the players
> of my youth on the grassy field below. There is magic in this moment,
> for when I open my eyes and see my sons in the place where my father
> once sat, I feel an invisible bond between our three generations, an an-
> chor of loyalty linking my sons to the grandfather whose face they never
> saw but whose person they have already come to know through this most
> timeless of all sports, the game of baseball.

◆ 4 ◆

Spalding, Spink, and the First Standard History of Baseball

Baseball historians generally recognize Albert G. Spalding's *America's National Game* as the first attempt at writing a standard history of baseball. In the introduction to a recent reprint of *America's National Game*, Benjamin Rader, author of his own history of baseball, claims that Spalding's book "remained the standard work on early baseball history until the 1960s and continues to this day to shape our understanding of baseball's early history." First published in 1911 by Spalding's own American Sports Publishing Company, *America's National Game* was drawn from the papers of Henry Chadwick, baseball's pioneer journalist and statistician, who was commissioned by Spalding, just before Chadwick's death in 1908, to write a history of baseball. When Chadwick's death prevented him from completing the task, Spalding took it upon himself to write "the simple story of America's National Game as I have come to know it."

Yet in the same year that Spalding was publishing his history of baseball and claiming he wrote the book only at the urging of a dying Chadwick, Alfred H. Spink, the founder of *The Sporting News*, was already releasing a second and enlarged edition of *The National Game,* his own attempt at a standard history of baseball. First published in 1910 by the National Game Publishing Company out of St. Louis, *The National Game* was also written at the urging of Chadwick and completed by Spink after Chadwick's death: "I had always looked to [Chadwick] to do the work which I am trying to do here, but he having failed I will try in my poor way to gather up the lost threads and place them together." Spink's introduction to the second edition of *The National Game* includes several excerpts from letters of support and gratitude from prominent baseball officials, including American League president Ban Johnson and National League president T. J. Lynch. The excerpt from Charles Comiskey's letter includes praise for Spink's book as "the only real and complete history of baseball ever written." Ban Johnson's letter proclaims *The National Game* as "the standard history of America's most attractive and popular pastime."

Despite the lavish praise for the publication of *The National Game,* Spink's history of baseball drifted into obscurity over the years and became a rare find for baseball book collectors. Spalding's *America's National Game,* however, continued to be reprinted (including twice in the last decade) and became the reference book on the early history of baseball for later standard histories of the game. The continuing popularity of *America's National Game* as a history of baseball, however, is curiously at odds with Spalding's own stated intentions in writing his book. Twice in his foreword to *America's National Game,* Spalding claims that he did not undertake the writing of a history of baseball: "I wish again emphatically to disavow any pretense on the part of this work as a 'history of baseball.'" Instead, he found himself engaged in writing a story, embellished with his own reminiscences, of baseball's beginnings, its early abuses and evils, and the salvation of the game by Organized Baseball.

Spalding's claim that *America's National Game* is more of a story, blending personal memories and historic scenes, than an actual history of baseball is well supported by the text of his book. Like Benjamin

Franklin's *Autobiography*, Spalding's *America's National Game* embellishes historical events with the rags-to-riches story of a founding father proud and even vain of his own success and eager to place his achievements within the context of important historical times. The book also strongly expresses Spalding's belief in the moral authority of the baseball magnate and the absolute separation of the governance of baseball off the field from its on-the-field production. As for its appeal as a story, *America's National Game,* while overwritten and overwrought, self-indulgent and self-serving, reads like an American fable of good struggling against and overcoming the forces of evil.

America's National Game opens with Spalding's paean to baseball as "distinctively American as to its nativity, its evolution, development, spirit, and achievements." After celebrating baseball as one of the purest expressions of America's democratic spirit and combative nature, Spalding begins his story appropriately with the narrative of baseball's origin as an American game. Spalding's proof for claiming baseball's "purely American origin" is the Mills Commission's unanimous decision and declaration in 1907 that "Base Ball had its origin in the United States" and that "the first scheme for playing it, according to the best evidence obtainable to date, was devised by Abner Doubleday, at Cooperstown, New York, in 1839." Avoiding the "vexed controversy" surrounding a committee appointed personally by Spalding to refute Henry Chadwick's claim that baseball evolved from the English game of rounders and ignoring his own role in providing anecdotal evidence to the committee in support of Doubleday as the inventor of baseball, Spalding presents the committee's decision as a righteous verdict and historical prologue to the story of baseball.

Spalding's historical narrative, which has become seminal to baseball's standard histories, traces the game's evolution from its primitive stages to the formation of the New York Knickerbockers, the first baseball club, by Alexander J. Cartwright in 1845, and the Cincinnati Red Stockings, the first professional baseball club, by Henry Wright in 1869, through its turbulent attempts to form baseball associations until the emergence of the National League in 1876, followed by the National Agreement in 1883 and its establishment of the reserve list, and finally the New National Agreement in 1903, which gave baseball its modern structure of National and American Leagues. The actual plot of Spalding's story of baseball's history begins, however, with the inspirational tale of how a democratic yet combative game, "born in the brain of an American soldier" and baptised in the "bloody days of our Nation's direst danger... healed the wounds of war" and became a beacon to patriots "lighting their paths to a future of perpetual peace." Baseball's own storied path, while occasionally diverted by accounts of Spalding's accomplishments as a goodwill ambassador for the game, is presented as a moral struggle between heroes of skill, courage, and vision and villains consumed by greed, dishonesty, and dissipation. To prove itself worthy as America's game and to win the respect and support of the American people, baseball had to overcome gambling and drunkenness and banish them from its playing fields and had to defeat and heal the internal strife of player rebellions and self-destructive ownership.

Once the narrative of *America's National Game* establishes its patriotic and moral perspective, Spalding, like Franklin in his *Autobiography,* exploits history to express his personal views on the importance of sound character and proper conduct. Just as Franklin admired Cotton Mather's Good Christian rowing to salvation with the oars of moral integrity and sound business practices, Spalding respected both the Good Ballplayer, highly skilled and fiercely competitive but clean-souled and fair-minded, and the Baseball Magnate, exploited, envied, and abused by players, press, and public but a "strong man among strong men" in his dedication to his team and his service to baseball. For Spalding, baseball holds its lofty position as America's national game not only because of the democratic and competitive nature of the game itself but also because of the skilled and honest performance of its players and the moral courage and sound business practices of its owners.

In *America's National Game* Spalding even serves up Organized

Baseball's defining moments when its founding fathers, first William A. Hulbert, then Spalding himself, had to save baseball from the corruption of the crooked player, the strife of its own civil war, and the greed of the selfish and unscrupulous owner. The first historical crossroads in Spalding's story of baseball comes in 1877, when Hulbert, the founder and now president of the fledgling National League, is confronted in his office during the dead of winter by James Devlin, one of four Louisville players banned from the league for throwing games. An eyewitness to the incident, Spalding describes the moment when Devlin, "a sorry looking specimen of humanity," dropped to his knees and uttered "a plea for mercy as might have come from one condemned to the gallows." Hulbert, earlier anointed by Spalding as "the man who saved the game," hands Devlin a fifty-dollar bill but "in tears" tells the banned ballplayer he is dishonest, untrustworthy, and will never be forgiven and reinstated as long as Hulbert is alive.

More than a decade after Hulbert banned the crooked ballplayer from baseball's playing fields, Organized Baseball had to be rescued again, this time by Spalding himself, first from the Brotherhood War in 1890 and later from the threat of Freedmanism in 1901. Fixed in his belief in the absolute division and separation of management and labor, Spalding describes the revolt of the National Brotherhood of Baseball Players against the reserve rule and their attempt to form a Players' League as nothing less than "a fight to the death." As chairman of the National League's War Committee, Spalding, quoting General Sherman's famous "war is hell," readily admits that baseball's integrity, including his own, took a back seat to lies to the public and manipulation of the press. He even admits to his own role in trying to bribe King Kelly with a ten-thousand-dollar check into deserting the Brotherhood and rejoining the National League, a bribe that Kelly, though always desperate for money, refused. When the Players' League collapsed after one season and its delegates approached Spalding, "bearing a flag of truce," he first insisted on the "unconditional surrender" of the Brotherhood, then, "not to be outdone by the hero of

Appomattox, whose terms I had appropriated, I agreed that we would furnish places for all the seceding players."

Having already styled himself as one of the founding fathers of Organized Baseball and as the victorious commanding general in baseball's own civil war, Spalding, in the last chapter of his story of baseball's history, presents himself as a baseball Moses leading the National League out of the threatened tyranny of Freedmanism and into the peaceful prosperity of the New National Agreement and the formation in 1903 of two Major Leagues operating under "mutual protective rules." When Andrew Freedman, the president of the New York Club, attempted to take control of baseball by forming a National League Trust and syndicating the operation of the game, Spalding took it upon himself to liberate baseball from Freedman's villainy. In a dramatic speech at the December 11, 1901, meeting of the National League Convention, Spalding charged Freedman and the owners under his control with plotting the death of the National League. Identifying Hulbert and himself as the league's "two fathers," Spalding first reminded the owners of baseball's unique history as "a distinctly American sport, suitable to the American character, played under the rules known to every American boy ten years of age." Further reminding them that the National League's own reputation rested upon the public's faith in their ability and determination to protect the integrity of the game, Spalding warned the owners that they were about to abrogate their moral responsibility as guardians of baseball by accepting Freedman's plan for syndication: "'I hope that some kind of argument, some words that I may utter here, will bring you to a realizing sense of the situation. The eyes of this Nation are upon you, and somehow or other the people have an idea that you are a band of conspirators, taking nothing but gate receipts.'"

After warning the owners of the threat of Freedmanism to baseball, Spalding, now the master politician, gained control of the National League's presidency through parliamentary maneuvering and, though he never received the necessary quorum of votes, was able to trade his resignation from the presidency he never held officially or legally for Freedman's resignation from ownership and his withdrawal from baseball. With his own role as founder and savior of baseball dutifully enshrined in the pages of *America's National Game,* Spalding concludes his story of baseball's history with a note of gratitude to Ban Johnson for standing by him "most royally" in his struggle against Freedmanism and a brief and surprisingly modest summary of the peace agreement between the established National League and the rival American League in 1903. His closing tribute, however, is for yet another father and savior of baseball, Henry Chadwick. After recognizing Chadwick as the inventor "of the first system of scoring and recording contests on the ball field" and as the person most responsible for professional baseball's "perfectly accurate records," Spalding reminds his readers one last time of the moral struggle to make baseball a "clean game" as well as a business success: "But it was not to Mr. Chadwick's love for Base Ball, great as it was; not to his ability as a writer, forceful and graceful as his literary efforts were ever acknowledged to be; not to his accuracy as a statistician, perfect as were his achievements along those lines; but to his indomitable energy and sublime courage in behalf of the integrity of Base Ball that our national game is most indebted for its high standing in the estimation of the American people."

With its glowing tribute to Chadwick, *America's National Game* completes its baseball pantheon and draws the curtain on Spalding's story of baseball's dramatic history. Out of Spalding's narrative of the democratic and combative game of baseball, from its fabled beginnings, through its moral struggles with gambling and greed, to its ultimate triumph as national pastime and business monopoly, emerges three great personages: the player, the fan, and the writer, but with the magnate always lurking benevolently behind the scene. In Albert G. Spalding, elected to the Hall of Fame in 1939, baseball has its Great Player, a pitcher of heroic performance on the playing field, who gave up his brilliant career to become the game's greatest organizer and promoter. In William A. Hulbert, finally elected to the Hall of Fame in 1995, baseball has its Great Fan, so devoted to the game that he spent his life serving as its staunchest defender and eventually as its savior. And in Henry Chadwick, elected to the Hall of Fame in 1938, baseball has its Great Writer, a journalist and historian who recognized the importance of statistics and records to the game but also wrote with grace and courage in support of baseball's value to the American people and its worthiness as America's national pastime.

America's National Game, even after its tribute to Chadwick, meanders on for fourteen more chapters, ranging in topics from college baseball to baseball literature and including more reminiscences and a closing interview, reprinted from the *New York Times,* in which Spalding equates the psychology of baseball to the psychology of success. As for baseball's future, it is inexorably linked to America's future: "So, like an endless chain, Base Ball will last and grow as long as these United States shall last and grow." For Spalding, the dream of playing baseball is synonymous with no less than the American Dream itself.

Yet, for all of Spalding's pontificating, the heart of *America's National Game* remains his story of the history of baseball, a history made up of all the ingredients of conventional storytelling: heroes and villains, melodramatic moments and moral cliff-hangers, and, of course, the expected happy ending with villains banished, heroes prospering, and baseball and its fans living happily ever after. While *America's National Game* may have become the standard work on early baseball for baseball's historians, its central narrative, inflated with self-serving reminiscences and patriotic and moral posturing, functions more as a story than as a documentary and reads better as a fabled history than as actual history.

◆ ◆

Alfred H. Spink's *The National Game* offers its readers a much more condensed and far less pretentious and melodramatic narrative of baseball history. Unlike Spalding in *America's National Game,* Spink in his foreword clearly declares that the goal of *The National Game* is "to present a faithful and accurate history of baseball, a history extending from the very time the game was first played up to the present moment." Instead of rendering baseball as a morally instructive and democratically inspiring tale of the triumph of the courageous, honest, and self-sacrificing magnate over greedy and crooked ballplayers, Spink's history records the accomplishments of "the great players who helped to bring the game into the prominence it now enjoys." Once it covers the major historical events in the evolution of Organized Baseball, *The National Game* devotes nearly half of its text to position-by-position biographical sketches of every current player in the National and American Leagues as well as many of those who played in earlier professional leagues. Its final hundred pages include sketches of managers, magnates, journalists, and umpires as well as a list of the players on every championship team from 1871 to 1900 and a complete record of all games played for championships from 1884 to the 1910 World Series. The last section of *The National Game* reprints an article by Charles Comiskey comparing the world championship teams of today with those of twenty-five years ago and includes Tim Murnane's booklet, *How to Play Baseball,* which contains essays from such baseball luminaries as Cy Young, Napoleon Lajoie, Hugh Jennings, and Fred Clarke.

Spink begins his history of baseball by stating that he "will not spend much time in referring to the birth of baseball." The first record or account of the game, according to Spink, was in 1830 "in the New England States," and the ball playing "in New England at this time much resembled the old game of 'town ball' played in England more than a century ago." The only mention of Abner Doubleday and Cooperstown in *The National Game* comes much later in a section on "The Game in New York," in which William Rankin, one of the most prolific baseball writers and historians of the time, dismisses the Cooperstown claim as a fake. In a March 13, 1909, letter to Spink, quoted in this section, Rankin, before making his own claim that baseball as an

American game "'owes its origin to Mr. Alexander J. Cartwright,'" takes on the Mills Commission report and what Spalding described as its righteous verdict: "'The latest of all the fakes was the one with the Cooperstown flavor in which one Abner Graves of Denver, Colo., declared that the late General Doubleday was its "designer and christener." He said he was a "kidlet" and was on the ground when General Doubleday turned the trick in 1839. What a pity for him he did not select some other year so that his air bubble could not have been pricked so easily. The records of West Point, N.Y., and the War Department at Washington, D.C., were the means of exposing his fake.'"

In his own opening commentary on the origins of baseball, Spink, in brief and concise sections, takes his readers through a description of the New England version of townball, the Philadelphia version developed by the Olympics in 1833, and eventually the "New York Game" originated by the Knickerbockers in 1845. Once Spink establishes the various claims for baseball's origins as an American game, he maps out a series of historical firsts, from the formation of the Knickerbockers, baseball's first real nine, in 1845 and the playing of the first match game in 1846 between the Knickerbockers and select New York clubs, to the first important series, the Fashion Race Course matches in 1858, and the first real series for a championship played on the Elysian Field in 1858 and 1859 between select clubs from New York and Brooklyn. After brief entries on other historical firsts—organization meetings, conventions, tours—Spink, after noting the expulsion in 1865 of James E. Roder from the Empire Club of New York "for accepting money for playing in one of its games," goes on to the growing professionalism of baseball, beginning with Spalding's Forest City Club of Rockford, Illinois, the first team to shift from paying players through the cooperative plan of providing jobs to paying regular salaries.

Shifting to baseball as a professional game, Spink now focuses on baseball's first great teams and its first great players. His entrees in *The National Game*, however, also begin to take note of growing problems with rowdyism and gambling as baseball becomes more and more popular. After an extended discussion of the formation and success-ful tour in 1869 of the Cincinnati Red Stockings, the first real team of paid professionals, a discussion punctuated by a photograph of the team taken in Washington by Mathew Brady, Spink notes that by 1875, despite the formation of the National Association of Players, "com-petition among the professional clubs ran so high that bribery, con-tract breaking, dishonest playing, poolroom manipulation and deser-tion of players became so public that the highly respectable element of patrons began to drop out of the attendance until the crowds which attended the games were composed almost exclusively of men who went to the grounds to bet money on the results."

Having arrived at the historical moment designated by Spalding in *America's National Game* as baseball's first crossroads, Spink, rather than serving up the melodramatic story of the confrontation between Hulbert and Devlin, places his historical discussion of the scandal within the formation of the National League in 1876 and its "relent-less war" against gambling that cleaned up the sport in just two years. He also gives a detailed account of the "Hartford Scandal" and the way Charles E. Chase, the president of the Louisville club, discovered and exposed the four players, including James Devlin, who had taken bribes from gamblers to lose enough of their final twelve games, in-cluding six against a weak Hartford club, to prevent Louisville from winning the National League pennant. Spink's only specific notice of Devlin is that he "pleaded for pardon at every league meeting til he died but the league had no pardon for this offense." Recognizing Devlin as one of the greatest pitchers of his era, Spink concludes with more detail than Spalding but with his own bit of moralizing: "For the sake of one hundred dollars—all the money Devlin got for the sale of these few games—he lost the ability to earn many thousands of dollars in later years and died absolutely in want. His fate and the fate of the three survivors of the quartet has been a lesson no ball player has ever forgotten."

Spink's account of the Brotherhood War of 1890, regarded by Spalding as another of baseball's moral mistakes and as a threat to its division of management and labor, is presented much more sympathetically and within a much broader context in *The National Game.* While recognizing the historical importance of the National Agreement of 1883 and its adoption and expansion of the 1880 reserve rule, Spink also claims that he has "always been the friend of the professional baseball players" and went with them "each time they set up in business for themselves." Accordingly, his section on the failed Union Association of 1884, the first player revolt against the National Agreement, is described as an attempt to "deliver the professional players out of bondage." The Brotherhood War, the most desperate revolt of the players against the reserve rule in the early history of baseball, is presented by Spink in the same military language as Spalding's account, but, after listing the opening-day batting orders for the Players' League, he lauds the players as "a lot of brave fellows" and sees the war leading to "a much better understanding between owners of the clubs and players and a respect for the latter's rights that had been conspicuous for its absence in certain places previous to the rebellion."

There is no mention of Freedmanism in *The National Game,* but Spink does allow Spalding his moment of self-promotion in the history of the National League by inserting part of an interview in which "Spalding tells in an interesting way of how the senior baseball organization of America was planned and built up." While Spalding's account of the formation of the National League is a shorter version of his chapter in *America's National Game,* the substance of his story remains the same—that the illegal signing of four players, including Spalding, from the Boston championship team by William Hulbert, the president of the Chicago Club, and their threatened expulsion from the National Association of Professional Baseball Players prompted Hulbert and Spalding to draft a constitution to form a new league and "to raise the standard of the game in every possible way." One of the unintended ironies of Spalding's story is that it precedes Spink's "interesting story" of the formation of the American League and his "claim to being the first" to suggest "an opposition association to the National League" and bring a new spirit of competition to professional baseball. Unlike Spalding's *America's National Game,* Spink's *National Game* gives a detailed account of the formation of the American League, from the early clandestine meetings in 1898 and 1899 and the reluctance of Ban Johnson to reorganize the Western League into the American League to the January 29, 1900, meeting in Chicago, where the new league, with the support of Johnson, Comiskey, McGraw, and others, was finally formed and, in spite of major opposition, became the equal of the National League in only a few years.

Spink's declaration of himself as the originator of the idea of a rival league to the National League and a major conspirator in the formation of the American League is a rare moment of self-aggrandizement in *The National Game,* and it anticipates another problem once Spink goes on to a history of baseball in the cities. Not surprisingly, considering Spink's St. Louis baseball roots, after listing the "pennant winning towns" and "the number of flags won" through 1909, he begins with a substantial section on the game in St. Louis, even though Chicago and Boston had won far more pennants. While the sections on New York and Chicago are also fairly substantial, the historical summaries tend to dwindle in space after the section on St. Louis, with the closing entries for cities like Pittsburgh, Baltimore, Brooklyn, Detroit, and Washington presented in less than one page.

Spink's St. Louis baseball roots are also apparent in the unusual frequency of St. Louis players in the position-by-position summaries for past and present players in the major leagues and in the presence of a high number of St. Louis personalities in some of his other biographical sections, such as those devoted to magnates and sportswriters. There are also several tributes paid to St. Louis personages in the various short essays in the last portion of *The National Game,* including Jeremiah Fruin, the father of baseball in St. Louis, Jack Ryan, a St. Louis hotel clerk "known by every professional baseball player as the greatest wit and best booster of the game living," St. Louisan Theodore

Breitenstein, the Cy Young of the minors, and the McNeary brothers, the first to build up baseball in St. Louis. Even the numerous photographs appearing throughout the book have a noticeable St. Louis tinge about them.

Yet for all the St. Louis coloring in *The National Game,* the sections on team histories, the biographical sketches, and the baseball features and anecdotes remain impressive in number and historical content. The hundreds of biographical sketches enhanced by nearly two hundred photographs provide a substantial look at the individual accomplishments and contributions of many of baseball's pioneers and also serve as indicators of the status and promise of baseball figures contemporary with the game in 1910. The sections of player sketches not only list the top yearly performance by position from 1871 to 1910, they also point out historical firsts for each position and often offer commentary on the performance and character of each player. They also at times include pieces of interviews published earlier in baseball magazines.

The length of each biographical sketch is usually determined by the stature of the player. There are extended entries for great players of the past, like King Kelly, Hoss Radbourn, and Cap Anson, and for established stars of the present, like Christy Mathewson, Honus Wagner, and Ty Cobb. There are also lengthy write-ups for rising stars, like Babe Adams, the Pittsburgh hero of the 1909 World Series, and a youthful Walter Johnson, as well as full treatments of the phenoms of the day, like Harry Krause of the Athletics, described by Connie Mack as the greatest left-hander to come into baseball since Rube Waddell, and Pittsburgh third baseman Bobby Byrne, who was "hitting like a fiend" in 1910 and was among the league leaders in batting average and runs scored.

There are biographical sketches that are surprisingly short and modest, like the entry for Wee Willie Keeler, or surprisingly critical, like the entries for Rube Marquard, faulted for his poor control and for not living up to his potential, and Sam Crawford, blamed for not running out hits of "the scratch kind." Other sketches sometimes euphemistically chide players for their poor physical condition or bad habits, the criticism often couched in terms of their "hefty" size or unexplained illness, though occasionally a player like Curt Welch, admired by Spink for his great outfield play for the St. Louis Browns in the 1880s, is openly condemned for being "a rough diamond, uncouth, uneducated."

Some of the more interesting and unusual sketches recognize the historical importance of key players in the evolution of baseball into the modern game or try to give the proper historical perspective to a player whose accomplishments have been overlooked. Arthur "Candy" Cummings, as expected, is acknowledged as the Father of the Curve Ball, but Alphonse "Phonnie" Martin, in a sketch that includes a commentary by Cummings on how he gripped and tossed the curve ball, is credited with being the first to pitch a slow curve "that nearly drove the batsman crazy and when he got ready to hit it good and hard it seemed to carrom away from him." Tommy Bond, taught the curve ball by Cummings, is recognized by Spink as "the first of the great speed pitchers and one of the first to throw the ball instead of to pitch it." Other historical firsts in Spink's biographical sketches include Nin Alexander, the first catcher to move up close to the batter, and Arthur Irwin, the first to use a fielder's glove. Other entries go into detail about the fielding prowess of Hal Chase, the ability of Ed Walsh to throw a spitball, and the leadership qualities of Frank Chance. There are sketches that stress the oddball and free-spirited nature of "Bugs" Raymond and his base dancing, Walter Latham and his clowning, and Dan O'Leary and his wrong-way sprint around the bases. Others draw out careers cut short or accomplishments never fully recognized or appreciated. There are the expected accounts of Jim Creighton's fatal injury and Ed Delahanty's mysterious death, but there is also the curious story of William Lange, described by Spink as a "Ty Cobb enlarged" and the last of the "individual idols," who gave up the game in his prime because of his bride's objections to baseball. Spink also uses his biographical sketches to remember the ambidextrous Fred

Dunlap, described as baseball's greatest second baseman, who died ignored and penniless, and Dutch Long, a shortstop sensation in the 1890s, whose death after years of poverty and illness prompted the first proposition of "a home for indigent players."

The biographical sections for managers, magnates, writers, and umpires are also filled with historical firsts and individual accomplishments, but the section of biographical sketches for baseball's players, numbering over five hundred entries and covering nearly half of the text, is the most distinguishing feature of *The National Game* and validates Spink's claim that the book was written "so that the names of those who helped to build up and make base ball the greatest of outdoor sports may never be forgotten." Spink had hoped that his history of "the National Game shall be continued for all time, with an addenda each year, so that the happenings of the game from its commencement up to the ever present period may be chronicled and kept close at hand." Unfortunately for Spink, the second edition of *The National Game* was the last update of his book and, unfortunately for baseball history, the last printing in the twentieth century.

Often reprinted, Spalding's story of baseball in *America's National Game* continues to entertain and influence our understanding of early baseball history, but Spink's *National Game,* despite its extensive documentation, its richly drawn sketches of the pioneers of baseball, and its amazing gallery of photographs, became so rare that even *The Sporting News* library lacks an original copy of the second and enlarged edition. While Spink's hope for an ever-expanding publication of *The National Game* proved vain after the second edition, his book merits at least equal status with Spalding's *America's National Game* as a valuable document of early baseball history and recognition as the first real attempt at a standard history of the game.

◆5◆

The Modern Historian's Game: Mixing Dream and Reality

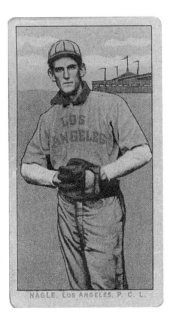

NAGLE, LOS ANGELES, P. C. L.

In 1960, nearly fifty years after the appearance of Spalding's *America's National Game* and Spink's *National Game*, Harold Seymour's *Baseball: The Early Years*, self-described as the first serious attempt to write a scholarly history of baseball, was published by Oxford University Press. In his preface to what was to become a multivolume history of baseball, Seymour claims that even though the "history of baseball's development is the story of nineteenth-century America in microcosm," baseball "has been badly served by history." Books purported to be authoritative merely "repeat the same tired legends and misinformation about baseball handed down, and copied uncritically, from one writer to another." Using "documentary evidence" instead of "invented conversations" and "stale anecdotes," Seymour's history will show with great detail and accuracy how baseball, in becoming a symbol for America, "added a new dimension to our economy, contributed color and flavor to our language, provided a theme for song, story, and stage, and supplied many names to the galaxy of American folk heroes."

In sharp contrast to Spalding's use of romance and mythology to justify the business of baseball to its fans and to herald the baseball magnate as the savior of the game, Seymour draws a clear distinction between baseball as business and baseball as religion. He establishes this distinction early in his narrative by dismissing Spalding's claims for Doubleday and Cooperstown as nothing more than the stuff of mythmaking. He then traces the beginnings of baseball to the English game of rounders and designates Alexander Cartwright and his Knickerbockers as the real founders of modern baseball. As for Organized Baseball's sanction of the Doubleday myth and the 1907 Mills Commission report on the American origin of baseball, Seymour simply notes that "the Commission was used to substantiate the very myth which it created in the first place. Of course, the fact that Organized Baseball 'gave official sanction' has no historical weight whatever."

In tracing baseball's historical development through its early or premodern years, Seymour follows the same storied path as Spalding, but instead of finding heroes and villains engaged in moral struggles for the soul of baseball, Seymour gives his historical attention and narrative weight to the more ironic account of the organization of baseball into a big business and its eventual emergence as a monopolistic enterprise. While recognizing the attempt of ownership to sell the game as "a symbol of democracy," Seymour sees baseball defined by the "undemocratic character of Organized Baseball's governmental structure," replete with territorial rights, blacklists, and the notorious reserve clause. In narrating a history of trade wars, player revolts, and ownership factionalism and mismanagement, Seymour offers baseball's readers a professional game too often characterized by hoodlumism and dirty play, a spectator sport too vulnerable to rowdy fans, pool sellers, and gamblers, and an undisguised monopoly plagued by shortsighted and opportunistic owners.

Yet even with its chaotic history and the often disruptive behavior of players, owners, and fans, baseball, in Seymour's narrative, still developed into the American National Game because of the physical pleasure and aesthetic joy of playing the game and its broad appeal as a spectator sport. With professional players improving the game's rules and performance, with spectators taking civic pride in their professional teams, with the commercialization of baseball benefitting from the dramatic increase in "America's march toward industrialism and urbanization," and with the press extolling the game as morally uplifting and transforming ballplayers into folk heroes, baseball, as it advanced into the modern age, "had won a permanent and significant place for itself on the American scene."

Placed beside Seymour's *Baseball: The Early Years*, Spalding's *America's National Game* reads more like propaganda than history, more like a how-to book on building a baseball monopoly while romanticizing one's actions as patriotic, heroic, and moral. Seymour's history, grounded in economics and free of the self-serving mythologizing and hero-making tendencies of Spalding's narrative, remains detached from the personalities of baseball's early years and relatively objective in describing the major events in baseball's evolution into the modern game. While Seymour does, at times, simplify baseball's early history into a cautionary tale of ruthless owners gaining monopolistic control over baseball and consigning its players to slavery, his narrative counters this tendency toward black-and-white moralizing with the recognition of the sound judgments and strong actions of Hulbert and others in getting baseball through decades of crises and controversies and with the acknowledgment of the brutish behavior of players and fans that constantly threatened baseball as it evolved into the national pastime.

In his second volume, appropriately titled *Baseball: The Golden Age*, Seymour takes his readers from the organization of baseball into the National and American Leagues in 1903 to the advent of Babe Ruth and his domination in the era of the 1920s. First published in 1971, a little more than a decade after Seymour's first volume on baseball's early years, *Baseball: The Golden Years* keeps its narrative focus, for the most part, on the major historical events that shaped Organized Baseball in the early decades of the twentieth century: baseball's economic boom in the gilded 1900s, epitomized by the construction of the first steel and concrete ballparks, the 1914 Federal League trade war, the 1919 Black Sox scandal and the resultant appointment in 1921 of baseball's first commissioner, the development of the minor-league farm system, and finally the radical shift in the 1920s from dead-ball play to a more spectacular game characterized by the home run. His overriding theme, however, is that as baseball went through radical changes on and off the field, fans became more emotionally attached to the game than ever: "They took their local team and their baseball seriously. The pennant races were exciting and important even to the countless Americans who had never been to a big-league game, and the famous players were important and real even to those who had never laid eyes on them. Ultimately, it was this profound emotional grip on the public that gave the game genuine vitality in the era from 1903 to 1930 and made it into a golden age."

This profound emotional grip is also evident in Seymour's own narrative of baseball's golden age. In his opening chapter he sets the stage for his history of baseball in the early decades of the twentieth century by drawing attention to the popular equation, at that time, of baseball with "Americanism, democracy, and the health and well-being of the young and old" and by endorsing Zane Grey's view that the game fulfilled "the American need for expression because it was open and manly, and full of risks, surprises, and glorious climaxes." Seymour's opening view that baseball was now ingrained "in the American psyche" finds its strongest expression in the "Hero and Heroics" section of his historical narrative. In chapters ranging from "The Making of a Hero" to "Stars and Galaxies," Seymour finds an emotional core for baseball history in the need of fans to create heroes, cloak them with traditional American values, and interpret their success on the field as proof that "storied American virtues actually paid off." To validate baseball as an American "*deus ex machina*," calling American boys from farms, towns, and cities and transforming them into heroes and legends, Seymour, though he tempers his narrative with reminders that baseball players are not gods, catalogs players, teams, and events that are so glittering, wondrous, and dramatic that they seem the stuff of dreams rather than history—"In a novel it would have been unbelievable."

The narrative of *Baseball: The Golden Years* is further emotionalized by Seymour's occasional use of personal reminiscences to highlight his historical account of Organized Baseball from 1903 to 1930. As the historical narrative progresses and moves closer to the time of his own youth, the instances of Seymour's recollection of his experiences as a batboy for Wilbert Robinson's Brooklyn club and his own emotional attachments as a Brooklyn fan come more and more into play. And the closer the narrative moves toward the teams and players of Seymour's youth, the more colorful and ardent the language becomes in describing the heroes of baseball's golden age. This narrative shift is most apparent in Seymour's tribute to the "notables" of the 1920s in his last chapter, where heroes are elevated to the mythical heights of best ever, while their human failings are romanticized as peccadillos. Seymour's readers are told, for example, that Paul Waner's "heavy drinking apparently relaxed him," and Hack Wilson "never begged off from playing because of a hangover."

This transformation of Seymour's narrative from a scholarly account of baseball's golden age to a nostalgic rendering of his own golden youth becomes obvious in the volume's final pages, when the focus shifts from a celebration of baseball's notables to a loving tribute to its most "colorful incapables," Brooklyn's "Daffiness boys." Once the transition from the scholarly to the more anecdotal and personal is complete, the narrative closes with an emotional tribute to Brooklyn baseball fans and their loyalty to their team and love of the game. As for Brooklyn boys like Harold Seymour, "Contact with baseball was therefore well-nigh inescapable. . . . They grew up in an environment pervaded by the game. Many opportunities to play it on sandlot and school teams beckoned them. Consequently generations of them became thoroughly imbued with baseball from earliest childhood. The game supplied a common interest that brought boys into a relationship that required them to judge one another primarily on merit and thereby helped them to develop mutual respect despite cultural differences."

Seymour's conclusion of his second volume, with its celebration of the physical and emotional appeal of baseball to boys and its connective and cohesive value to generations of fans, anticipates the content and direction of his next volume: *Baseball: The People's Game*. In the preface to *Baseball: The Golden Years,* Seymour had stated his intention to write a third book "that will carry the story forward to the present" and include "discussion of the important and long-neglected role of black Americans in baseball." Instead, as he acknowledges in the preface to *Baseball: The People's Game,* Seymour decided to end his work on the history of Organized Baseball and become the first scholar "to present a comprehensive account of baseball outside of Organized Baseball."

Rather than the promised historical extension of his first two volumes on Organized Baseball from its beginnings to 1930, Seymour's final volume becomes a complement to his earlier work, a study of the entire structure of baseball from its early years through its golden age. Using the metaphor of baseball as a house of many layers and tenants and consigning Organized Baseball to the top floor and the Hall of Fame to the attic, Seymour begins *Baseball: The People's Game* with several chapters on the "foundation" of baseball, its boys' teams: "for only in boyhood and youth can skills in playing the game and, more important, love of it be developed." Once establishing boys' baseball as the foundation of his House of Baseball, Seymour goes on to complete his primary structure by designing a "ground floor" out of chapters on the college game, town teams, industrial players and leagues, the semipros and traveling or barnstorming teams like the House of David, armed forces play in America and overseas, and even "the game's lusty offspring, eventually to be known collectively as softball." With his primary structure in place, Seymour completes his house by first constructing a "basement" for his rather curious coupling of "American Indians" with convicts, juvenile delinquents, and "mental defectives," then, in an unwitting mockery of Virginia Woolf's "A Room of One's Own," adding an "annex" for baseball's women players, before finally and unfortunately finishing the House of Baseball with an "outbuilding" for its black players.

Despite the strained extension and eventual rhetorical collapse of Seymour's metaphor of the House of Baseball, the narrative of *Baseball: The People's Game* provides readers with a highly detailed account of the richly various layers of the game being played beneath the stratum of Organized Baseball. Seymour's narrative also casts a cold eye on problems inherent in baseball's evolution into the national pastime, ranging from the bureaucratic takeover of boys' baseball and the administrative conversion of college baseball into a cash cow to the exclusion of Native Americans, women, and African Americans from baseball's main enterprise because of myths of inferiority, subordination, and segregation. Yet Seymour's own narrative enterprise, as ironic and judgmental as it is in exposing the social and economic corruption and moral failure within the structure of baseball, still encloses itself within the romantic vision of baseball as a game for innocents and the stuff of dreamy anecdotes for adults: "Boys rarely leave documentary evidence of their baseball days until youth passes. Then a few of them, the author of this book included, peer through the soft mists of memory and record their boyhood experiences."

Seymour's final volume of his baseball history, much like the conclusion of his previous volume on baseball's golden age, certainly peers through the soft mists of memory, especially in its opening section and its often anecdotal tribute to a boys' baseball that is expressive of the American virtues of individual courage and sportsmanship and played on sandlots and cow pastures with taped baseballs and mended bats. Though Seymour's main historical narrative is often ironic, his own vision of baseball best expresses itself in the delight of watching a big-league game or the joy of reading juvenile fiction with its larger-than-life heroes and its double curves and magical bats. Seymour finds baseball's own best character in its democratic capacity to assimilate ethnic groups into American culture and to give boys an opportunity to develop their own character through the natural act of playfulness. For Seymour, the game of baseball more than anything else gives American boys what they need: "time to escape, to be let alone, to be themselves, to experience and learn on their own at their own pace and through informal play in free association with their fellows, where they could test themselves, gauge their friends, make decisions, commit mistakes, exercise imagination, improvise, give and take (lumps included), and experience a lot more that comes under the rubric of social, emotional, and moral growth."

Seymour's abiding belief in boys' baseball as the foundation for baseball's claim to the title of America's pastime, his anecdotal injection of his own baseball memories into his scholarly historical narrative, and his romantic vision of baseball as democratic in spirit and play link Seymour's three-volume history, despite its disclaimer, to A. G. Spalding's *America's National Game* and its claim that baseball begins with a boy and a ball and its celebration of the game as democratic and combative in nature. Seymour's vision and memories also place his historical narrative within the broad context of traditional baseball writing and its dream narrative and further link it to anecdotal histories, like Joseph Durso's *Baseball and the American Dream,* that are unabashedly romantic in character. More than anything else, however, Seymour's historical narrative, with its eventual and seemingly inevitable blending of romance and memory with scholarly details and ironic commentary, anticipates the consistent dilemma for the baseball scholar determined to write a standard history of baseball but acutely aware of and vulnerable to the pervasive influence of the mythic trappings and the dreamy lure of the game.

Six years after the appearance of the first volume of Harold Seymour's history of baseball, *American Baseball: From the Gentlemen's Sport to the Commissioner's System,* the first book in David Quentin Voigt's multivolume history, was published by the University of Oklahoma Press. His second volume, *American Baseball: From the Com-*

missioners to Continental Expansion, appeared in 1970, the same year as the second volume of Seymour's history. Voigt's final volume, *American Baseball: From Postwar Expansion to the Electronic Age,* was published by the Pennsylvania State University Press in 1983, along with reprints of Voigt's first two volumes.

Voigt's three-volume history of baseball has been described by Mike Shannon in *Diamond Classics* as "the most thorough and comprehensive history of baseball ever published." Though its first volume is no more detailed or comprehensive in its historical narrative of Organized Baseball from its beginnings to 1903 than Seymour's *Baseball: The Early Years,* a book barely acknowledged by Voigt, the next two volumes justify Shannon's claim for comprehensiveness, or at least greater coverage of Organized Baseball, in Voigt's multivolume history. The second volume of *American Baseball,* for example, while focusing on Seymour's "golden age" from 1903 to 1930, also takes baseball through its survival years during the Depression and World War II to the beginning of its "Mid-century Upheaval." Voigt's third volume follows baseball through its boom years of the 1950s and the beginnings of expansion in the 1960s to the plastic and electronic age of the 1970s and the dawning of free agency.

While five additional decades of baseball history certainly distinguish Voigt's multivolume work from Seymour's, the historical narrative of *American Baseball* also differs significantly in its approach, which is far more sociological, and in its perspective, which is far more given to baseball's cult of personality. After prefacing his first volume with Johan Huizinga's thesis in *Homo Ludens* that "fun is a basic need of man" and his own claim for the nineteenth century in America as the beginning of a leisure revolution, Voigt sends his historical narrative down a now-familiar path by first noting then dismissing the Cooperstown myth, before discussing baseball's emergence from amateur ball into a professional sport. Rather than seeing baseball's early history as a series of economic events, Voigt's view, while it recognizes baseball's creeping commercialism, tends to focus, like Spink's *National*

Game, on the personages of the game. His discussion of baseball's true origins is grounded in his appreciation of Henry Chadwick's historical role as baseball's first "leading authority and critic on baseball matters," which, in turn, anticipates the essential role that sportswriters will play in the narrative of *American Baseball.* Voigt's story of baseball's first professional team and its first professional league is highlighted by a tribute to Harry Wright as a symbol of "the best of the gentleman's era," just as Spalding is to epitomize "the values of rugged commercialism" and Hulbert the myth of baseball as a moral force.

When his narrative reaches the critical historical juncture of the formation of the National League and the subsequent transition of power from players to owners that began "the modern era of major league baseball," Voigt shifts his narrative attention to the emergence, with the considerable help of sportswriters, of baseball players, ironically now stripped of their freedom by the reserve clause, as America's new heroes. In setting up the 1880s as the first golden age of baseball, he introduces the decade, otherwise characterized by a trade war that laid the groundwork for a player revolt, with the story of Adrian "Cap" Anson, the "prototype of the new hero-player." His section on the golden age of baseball culminates with chapters on baseball as if it were more the stuff of drama and fiction than history. His "Baseball's Cast of Characters" chapter includes baseball players newly defined as heroes and even superstars; fans elevated to a baseball chorus capable of praising and condemning their heroes; umpires made villainous and damned as "a universal symbol of hate"; and sportswriters expressing themselves at times as critics but more often as "yarn spinners" and tellers of "colorful tall stories." His chapter on baseball's coming of age, while noting the game's growth into Big Leagues and its players into Big Leaguers, celebrates baseball as a permanent expression of America's "dominant national values" and a dynamic display, in its improvements in equipment and use of technology, "of our national faith in machinery and gadgets."

Voigt ends his first volume with historical accounts of baseball's turbulence throughout the 1890s and its eventual return in the first decade of the twentieth century to the stability and prosperity of the 1880s, but his historical focus stays on the personages of the game. His narrative of the 1890s is really the story of two moral struggles, one between robber barons, headed by Andrew Freedman, and gentleman-owners, led by A. J. Reach, for the control of the baseball enterprise; the other between the brawling and rowdy play of the "manly game" and the clean and legitimate style of the "scientific game" for control of baseball's playing field. His closing tale of baseball's return to stability and prosperity is highlighted by a tribute to Ban Johnson, who became baseball's first Olympian ruler, hurling "his thunderbolts at players, umpires, and owners" until his passing ended baseball's silver era.

The historical narrative of Voigt's second volume remains even more firmly in the emotional grip of baseball's tendency to glorify its eras and deify its players. The narrative at times even surrenders its own rhetoric to the exaggerated and jargonized language of baseball's hero worship and mythmaking. Voigt's sections and chapters on the history of baseball from the beginning of its modern era in 1903 to its midcentury upheaval and the dawn of the "Plastic Age" are filled with celebratory accounts of baseball's silver age and its second golden age, of dead-ball dynasties and Yankee domination, and of heroes and demigods. Voigt's own exaggerated writing and stilted language transforms the dead-ball era Ty Cobb both into "the Lancelot of [his] age" and "the hot-tempered devil of baseball." The latter-day Lou Gehrig becomes the "Galahad of [his] era" and the personification of "the Protestant ethic in baseball." Branch Rickey, one of Voigt's "demigods," is mythologized into baseball's Vulcan because, with the invention of the farm system, he "made the weapons for the other gods." Among baseball's celebrated sportswriters, Ring Lardner, with his understanding of the "dark side" of baseball, is eulogized as the "Voltaire" of his age.

Voigt's hyperbolic prose is also capable of giving biblical proportions to team triumphs and converting team disgrace into tragedy. For Voigt, the 1906 World Series victory of the "hitless wonders" Chicago White

Sox over the titanic Chicago Cubs rivals David and Goliath as a "Sunday School lesson" for American children. The 1919 World Series fix, thanks to Hugh Fullerton's determined reporting, compared by Voigt to "lifting the lid on the Pandora's box," began as a "tangled tale of corruption" but eventually was elevated in the public's mind to "an American tragedy." Voigt's explanation of the Yankee domination of baseball's second golden age ranges from the Gothic vision of Harry Frazee as a baseball Faust selling Babe Ruth and presumedly baseball's soul to the demonic New York Yankees to the talismanic power of pinstripe uniforms, an idea credited to Douglass Wallop, whose own devil in *The Year the Yankees Lost the Pennant* actually hates the Dodgers more than he loves the Yankees.

At the conclusion of the second volume of his baseball history, Voigt, lamenting the "death of [baseball] gods" like Babe Ruth, notes the absence of heroic or godlike qualities in the new breed of players at midcentury: "their personalities were rather dull, and none had the radiance of a Cobb or Ruth." At the same time, however, his final vision of baseball as it headed into the second half of the century is favorable and even optimistic because of the game's energetic, flexible, and innovative character. This ambivalence carries over into Voigt's third volume, though he has no trouble finding new heroes, villains, and even an emancipator to dot the landscape of baseball's turbulent and controversial historical journey through the last decades of the twentieth century, an era marked by franchise shifts, league expansion, free agency, strikes and lockouts and, above all else, the electronic selling of the game.

Voigt's overriding view in his third volume is that the game of baseball became plastic in its look, though "plastic" for Voigt also "conveys a sense of creativity, an ability to adapt to change." As for the new breed of ballplayers and their pursuit of wealth instead of the baseball dream, these "newly minted . . . plutocrats," for all their posturing, also worked like "an aphrodisiac" for the newly adoring baseball fans who flocked to the ballparks. Allowing itself its own good measure of creativity and adaptability, Voigt's narrative adds in celebrity heroes like Reggie Jackson, bestriding the baseball world "as a colossus," "chipmunk" sportswriters replacing the "giant tortoises" of the past and digging into the private lives of celebrity heroes, "bad animal" fans and their "victory riots," newly unionized and militant umpire "villains," "scapegoat" managers unable to control and discipline the new celebrity breed of ballplayers, and "robber baron" owners plagued by "self-made problems," especially their own inflated egos.

Voigt's historical narrative is also characterized by the same rhetorical embellishments and distractions that appear in his second volume. Historical events and personages routinely take on literary and religious trappings. The story of Jackie Robinson's crossing of the major-league color line, while dispelling "popular myths of black stupidity," becomes "an American morality play." Don Larsen's perfect game in the 1956 World Series is not only "an Olympian event," it suggests "divine intervention" on baseball's playing fields. When baseball enters its expansion era, Walter O'Malley appears as "the first Lord of baseball," its master expansionist, though as an "evolutionary throwback to the robber baron owners of the 1890s" probably "the last of a doomed species, a baseball Brontosaurus." What baseball required, as Voigt's narrative culminates in the postmodern electronic age with its plastic ballparks, celebrity ballplayers, and worshipful but demanding fans, was a new breed of leader, a rebel for a new age and no less than a baseball Emancipator. For Voigt that charismatic figure is Marvin Miller, whose skill in labor laws and courage in confronting "avenging owners" liberated baseball's players and envisioned the game, as it entered the last decades of the twentieth century, as a utopia "governed by a council representing all the games's constituencies."

While Voigt closes his three-volume history with a rosy vision of a postmodern baseball world rooted in its "elegant past," strong in its "historical continuity," and inherently capable of adapting itself to new challenges and finding new leadership, later histories have had trouble accepting Voigt's optimism and faith in baseball as the national pastime. These later works are also representative of a major shift in baseball's historical narratives from the standard history, often colorized by baseball lingo and legend for fan appeal, to an academic biography, written from a more moderate and restrained perspective for the student of baseball. These academic biographies, less personal and value-driven, also tend to offer helpful bibliographical essays surveying the field of baseball's historical writing and even occasionally acknowledge and quote other historians in their narrative text.

Charles Alexander's *Our Game: An American Baseball History,* despite its colorized title, is one of the best examples of the trend in baseball's historical narratives toward balance and self-restraint. While acknowledging in his preface that much of what he knows about baseball "comes from personal observation and recollection—in other words, from being a fan," Alexander also states that, as a baseball historian, he sought to maintain a balance between anecdote and interpretation and details and explanation: "I wanted to cover the history of baseball—as game, sport, business, and social institution—in a way that would interest baseball-lovers of all kinds, be sound enough to satisfy specialists, and prove serviceable as a compact, inclusive, one-volume history." As for narrative treatment, "history ought to be narrated in real time, which means giving some sense of the crowded, disordered nature of the past."

With only a few exceptions, Alexander's one-volume history of baseball from the 1830s to the beginning of the 1990s lives up to its stated intentions. Its narrative provides baseball readers with a compact, serviceable chronicle of baseball that clearly presents and discusses great players and major events within the context of their own time. Narrated in "real time," Alexander's history first follows baseball from its amateur days "as a form of play for men who weren't really athletes and weren't trying to be" through its capricious development into a professional sport, to its eventual emergence, after an era of disorderly conduct on and off the field, as a business monopoly and the national pastime. Once "modern baseball" begins, ironically with a "dead-ball era," Alexander's narrative methodically follows it through crowded, controversial decades filled with player scandal and banishment, individual and team greatness and accomplishment, economic depression and social controversy, structural and technological expansion and advances, and eventually the economic and political changes that have brought baseball to its current state of "periodic player-owner impasses and disruptions of the sport's seasonal cycle," caused by the irrational behavior of "rapacious, pigheaded owners" and the players' "insatiable money demands." As for baseball's future and future interest in the game: "What it all came down to finally, was whether one was willing to put up with the trials and travails that went with being a baseball fan near the end of the twentieth century."

As Alexander tells the story of baseball, his narrative stays relatively free of the stilted and jargonized language, the mythical allusions, romantic allegories, and moral imperatives, and the dramatic and sometimes melodramatic claims that are frequent mannerisms of baseball histories. Alexander's narrative, while it accepts the conventional characterizations of players as "serfs," ball clubs as "medieval fiefdoms," and baseball's best decades as "golden," avoids the standard perception of baseball's great players and performances as transcendental and transformative. Instead of dressing up baseball in its mythic trappings and surrounding the game with the aura of the dream, Alexander presents baseball history's key players and events within the dimensions of their own playing time. This strategy of framing baseball's greatness within a tightly fitted chronology not only creates the impression of a narrative moving through real time, it gives Alexander the opportunity to show how certain moments in baseball, because of their historical position, have taken on the qualities of folklore and mythology and certain players, because of their emotional and imaginative impact on their own era, have taken on the trappings of legends and immortals for following generations. Alexander's historical narrative is well aware of baseball's timeless appeal, but he sees this timelessness emanating from time itself or, for the baseball historian, from time past.

Another quality of Alexander's *Our Game* that further enhances its sense of compactness, inclusiveness, and serviceability is its integration of black baseball within its historical narrative. Acknowledging the pioneering work of Robert Peterson's *Only the Ball Was White* and anticipating the integrated narrative of Ken Burns's popular television series on baseball, Alexander, rather than consigning black baseball to an historical outhouse or annex, places its history within the chronology of his American baseball history. The result is a narrative that integrates its own history of baseball long before Jackie Robinson crossed baseball's color line and began the slow process of the integration of Organized Baseball.

Alexander's *Our Game* has advanced the baseball historical narrative from the standard fan's history of baseball to a more studied approach to baseball's past in which the temporality rather than the timeless appeal of baseball becomes its most prominent feature. This new historical approach, rather than drawing attention to the historian's anecdotal relationship with baseball or his own emotional attachment to the game, keeps the narrative focus on baseball's relationship to its own past and the emotional, moral, and dramatic context of each decade or era of baseball's history. The new baseball historian takes Jacques Barzun's often quoted claim that "whoever wants to know the heart and mind of America had better learn baseball" and gives weight and credibility to Barzun by adding the word "history" to his celebrated quotation.

One of the best examples of the attempt to give baseball history a sense of its own past is Benjamin G. Rader's *Baseball: A History of America's Game*. Rader's book is further distinguished by its recognition of the contributions of earlier historical narratives. In his acknowledgments he states that, after years of doing "serious" research as a professional historian, he turned to the history of baseball because of the pioneering "research and thoughts of others." While acknowledging an impressive group of historians, ranging from Seymour and Voigt to Goldstein and Alexander, he gives fuller recognition by often quoting or summarizing the work of others in his own historical narrative. He also offers a concluding bibliographical essay that summarizes the major historical works on baseball and places them into appropriate general categories: the nineteenth century; 1900–1950; and the post-1950 era. His categories also include a breakdown of historical narratives into subcategories and subtopics ranging from team histories to histories of single years and individual events.

Rader's own historical narrative of baseball, rather than dismissing the nostalgia and hyperbole of past histories of "legendary players and teams," attempts to bring the epic accounts of "what took place on the playing field" into "a broader story" of the historical development of baseball's own culture and its social relationship with the ambitions and aspirations of the American people. By incorporating baseball's epic history into his account of the real history of baseball, Rader is able to exploit baseball's tendency to mythologize its past and romanticize the playing of the game to give his own historical narrative a sense of vividness and drama. He also enriches his narrative by re-creating a sense of place at the beginning of each chapter of his chronicle and noting the larger historical circumstances surrounding a major event in the development of baseball's cultural and social history.

His chapter on the first professional leagues, for example, begins with the re-creation of the moment William A. Hulbert, meeting on February 2, 1876, with the representatives of six eastern ball clubs, locked the delegates in a Manhattan hotel room until they agreed to sign a pact creating the National League. Rader then notes that this meeting, eventful to "baseball's claim to the national pastime . . . took place during the nation's centennial year of 1876" and that league play began in the same spring that General Custer and his troops were massacred at Little Big Horn. His chapter on the baseball war that led to the formation of Organized Baseball in 1903 and launched baseball into its modern era opens with the informal meeting at dinner between Ban Johnson and a committee of owners from the National League to arrange the terms of a peace treaty that, as the revised National Agreement, would provide baseball with a major-league structure of teams good for the next fifty years. In his chapter on the Black Sox scandal he places "The Big Fix" within the historical context of the "Red Scare" and the presidential election of 1920 between James Cox and Warren Harding, who was surrounded by his own cloud of scandal and corruption when he died in office in 1923; but Rader also notes that the baseball scandal crowded "every other story off the front pages of the nation's newspapers." Subsequent chapters on "An Age of Dynasties," "Baseball's Great Experiment," and "The Last Days of the Old Game" all begin with dramatic moments: Grover Cleveland Alexander's strikeout of Tony Lazzeri in the 1926 World Series; Jackie Robinson's August 28, 1945, meeting with Branch Rickey; and Don Larsen's perfect game in the 1956 World Series, "the last ever played in New York City between the two great dynastic rivals of the post–World War II era."

The last chapter of Rader's history of baseball, after its narrative traces baseball's financial problems, organizational confusion, labor troubles, and player scandals of its most recent decades, closes on a more optimistic note than Alexander's by drawing attention once again to baseball's own nostalgia and the resiliency of the game. Yet Rader's concluding evocation of baseball's nostalgia and his insistence on the game's resiliency, while reminders of Spalding's romancing of baseball's early history, does not detract from his overall narrative with its synthesis of the work of other historians and its ability to place players and events within the dramatic and emotional context of their own time. Rader's history, if taken together with the work of Alexander, raises the standard for baseball's historical narratives, one that posits compactness, inclusiveness, mediation, and self-restraint as the conditions for historical writing and baseball's own temporality as the primary aim and ultimate achievement of the baseball historian.

◆ 6 ◆

Only Fairy Tales: Baseball Fiction's Short Game

BROWN VERNON. P. C. L.

In Mark Harris's *The Southpaw*, Henry Wiggen, rookie phenom, budding author, and the novel's narrator, asks a sportswriter why no one has written a decent book about baseball. When told there have been dozens of good books, Wiggen replies: "There has been only fairy tales."

Wiggen's brief moment as literary critic merely reflects the tendency of baseball fiction, including the short story, to mix fantasy with fact, the improbable with the probable, and to serve up this extraordinary blend as the ordinary and the routine. Over the decades, writers of baseball fiction have often squeezed the reality out of their narratives by creating a succession of outlandish or heroic characters acting out unlikely or fantastic plots. Often told from the first-person point of view, a perspective Henry James once described as a romantic privilege because of its tendency toward narrative looseness, baseball stories are routinely played out on the fields of the grotesque, supernatural, or metaphysical. Stripped of the incredible, their narratives usually flatten out, their characters becoming cardboard cutouts, their plots sentimental, their conflicts resolved by the conventional three-two-pitch, bottom-of-the-ninth, final-game-of-the-series-or-season moment of truth.

In Jim Shepard's "Batting against Castro," first published in *The Paris Review* and reprinted in *The Best American Short Stories of 1994*, there appears to be little connection between the realities of baseball and the fictional world of the story, beyond the debt of inspiration the narrative owes to a short essay by Don Hoak and Myron Cope about Fidel Castro and the Cuban Leagues: "It was there I learned that Castro actually came out onto the field and inserted himself as a relief pitcher to face Hoak in the winter of 1950–51. It was also there that I found various details for my story: the names of the contending clubs, the yellow tails and eels on the coral reefs, the fact that Batista himself witnessed the demonstrations at the games, and finally Castro's dress shirt and slacks. The image, the premise of Castro on the mound, seemed both irresistibly silly and filled with implication."

Irresistibly silly and filled with political implications is also an apt description of "Batting against Castro," a story not about Don Hoak, who didn't play in the major leagues until 1954, but about two inept Philadelphia Phillies playing out the end of their careers on a woeful 1951 team. Told by one of the players in a voice described by Shepard as "invincibly ignorant and vaguely hapless," the narrative reads like a Lardnersque baseball yarn about two banjo-hitting, politically incorrect lunkheads, the worst ballplayers on a team so pitiful it resembles the 1961 Phillies, losers of 107 games, including a record twenty-three in a row, rather than a ball club one year removed from winning the National League pennant. Shepard's baseball boobs are so awful that, after finishing the season in the minor leagues, they end up playing winter ball in Cuba in a futile attempt to salvage their careers. Once in Cuba, they play out their roles in an outlandish plot, made even more outrageous by all the prerevolutionary madness, which reaches its climax when Fidel Castro comes out of the stands to pitch to Shepard's woeful heroes at the moment of truth in the season's final and championship-deciding game.

A wonderfully written and entertaining story, "Batting against Castro" takes full advantage of the tendency of baseball fiction to serve up fantastic plots with exaggerated characters. Shepard's short story also, however, playfully subverts this tendency by making fun of the narratives of baseball fiction while at the same time claiming narrative authority from the oddities of baseball history itself. This artistic ambidexterity is most evident in the curious verisimilitude of the story's details and statistics and in the wild send-off at the story's conclusion. On the way to its extravagant ending, the narrative not only drops off cold-war signposts (the H-bomb, Korean War, and Dag Hammarskjöld) that point to its political implications, it also validates its hapless-hitting baseball characters with statistics from *The Baseball Encyclopedia.* The anemic .143 batting average of Shepard's narrator corresponds exactly with the record of Jimmy Bloodworth, an aging utility infielder whose batting and slugging average was .143 with the 1951 Phillies. The narrator's baseball sidekick, Charles Owen Caddell, old C.O.C. or "Can o' Corn," who, according to the narrator, batted his weight for the season, has his counterpart in 170-pound Dick Whitman, a .118 hitter for the 1951 Phillies. As for the narrator's struggling Phillies, twenty-three games out of first place late in the season, they actually do compare with the 1951 Phillies, a team that finished twenty-three-and-a-half games behind the pennant-winning New York Giants, despite having won the National League pennant the year before.

While the unlikely performances in "Batting against Castro" are actually mocking echoes of statistics in *The Baseball Encyclopedia,* the narrative's outrageous conclusion owes more to baseball fiction than to baseball history, though it serves more as send-up than as homage. The vision of Castro pitching to two inept members of the 1951 Phillies at the deciding moment of the Cuban League season is the extravagant stuff of baseball fiction writers from Lardner to Malamud and Kinsella, though Shepard's encounter owes more to Lardner's bushers and boobs than to Malamud's mythic natural and Kinsella's supernaturals. After the narrator is hit on the hip by a Castro change-up to load the bases, Caddell tries to duck away from a curve ball, but the ball hits his bat and dribbles back to Castro, who throws the ball into right field:

> Pandemonium. Our eighth and ninth hitters scored. The ball skipped away from the right fielder. I kept running. The catcher'd gone down first to back up the throw. I rounded third like Man o' War, Charley not far behind me, the fans spilling out onto the field and coming at us like a wave we were beating to shore. One kid's face was a splash of spite under a Yankee hat, a woman with large scars on her neck was grabbing for my arm. And there was Castro blocking the plate, dress shoes wide apart, Valentino pants crouched and ready, his face scared and full of hate like I was the entire North American continent bearing down on him.

As Shepard's narrator heads for home plate and his politically charged collision with Fidel Castro, the narrative has completely blurred the line between history and anecdote and between baseball facts and baseball fiction. Yet, as "Batting against Castro" has its fun with the intertextuality of reality and fantasy in baseball fiction, it also plays into a paradoxical narrative tradition of seeing baseball, despite its statistical dominion, as a metaphor for life and its players as larger than life. As for verisimilitude, unless it serves as comic relief, it often appears sadly out of key with the transformative power of baseball fiction, a power consistent with the vision of baseball as timeless and perfect.

In Robert Coover's metafictional "McDuff on the Mound," the powerful grip of the fabulous and the mythical on baseball fiction turns the narrative of Coover's short story into a nightmare for the pitcher in baseball's most annotated, anthologized, and immortalized literary event. Though not much more than a piece of baseball doggerel, Ernest L. Thayer's "Casey at the Bat" was granted mythic status as America's baseball classic as early as A. G. Spalding's *America's National Game:* "Love has its sonnets galore; War its epics in heroic verse; Tragedy its sombre story in measured lines; and Base Ball has 'Casey at the

Bat.'" Since then the poem has been celebrated, imitated, extended, and even parodied by writers and artists ranging from Grantland Rice to W. P. Kinsella. In discussing baseball's best poetry, Donald Hall claims "Casey at the Bat" as "the sentimental favorite" of America's poets and the best-known of all of baseball poems: "Everybody knows 'Casey at the Bat.'"

In Coover's "McDuff on the Mound," poor McDuff finds himself pitching in a cartoon version of "Casey at the Bat" in which some malevolent force appears to be manipulating the game so that McDuff has to face the mighty Casey. While McDuff, "a practical man with both feet on the ground," desperately holds on to his belief that he's pitching in a real game and can escape the fate of pitching to Casey, the Disney-inspired antics of Flynn and Blake, the rule book's statement that "anything can happen in Mudville," and the mythic dimensions and composure of Casey himself all lead McDuff to the revelation that he is merely the instrument in a ritual whose ultimate meaning is beyond his comprehension. But he at least knows by narrative's end that, all along, his role in the ritual is to face the mighty Casey:

> And Casey: who *was* Casey? A Hero to be sure. A Giant. A figure of grace and power, yes, but wasn't he more than that? He was tall and mighty (omnipotent, some claimed, though perhaps, like all fans, they got a bit carried away), with a great moustache and a merry knowing twinkle in his eye. Was he, as had been suggested, the One True Thug? McDuff shook to watch him. He was ageless, older than Mudville certainly, though Mudville claimed him as their own. Some believed that "Casey" was a transliteration of the initials "K.C." and stood for King Christ. Others, of a similar but simpler school, opted for King Corn, while another group believed it to be a barbarism for Krishna. Some, rightly observing that "case" meant "event," pursued this reasoning back to its primitive root, "to fail," and thus saw in Casey (for a case was also a container) the whole history and condition of man, a history perhaps as yet incomplete.

"Batting against Castro" and "McDuff on the Mound," if taken together, are delightfully wicked spoofs of the high seriousness of *The*

Baseball Encyclopedia and the timeless appeal of "Casey at the Bat," sacred texts that have, the one through recorded statistics and the other through singsong rhyme, transformed a weak-hitting utility infielder and the sentimental hero of a popular ballad into baseball immortals. Yet, while usurping an aging, anemic Jimmy Bloodworth and the ageless, mighty Casey for their own comic intent, Shepard and Coover, even as they undermine the sacred in baseball history and literature, also illustrate the way baseball stories convert the most mundane realities of baseball into fables and transform the occasional heroic or tragic act into romance. Even as they playfully mock the sacred and the nostalgic in baseball's narrative tradition, the short stories of Shepard and Coover, with their own exaggerated narratives, join that tradition and, while they may practice the art of parody, also corroborate the view expressed by W. P. Kinsella that baseball "is the most literary of sports" and, with its wonderful silences and open-endedness, is perfect "for larger-than-life characters, for the creation of myths and mythology."

The tradition of baseball stories with larger-than-life characters playing out their adventures on Elysian fields has its roots in the dime novel and the series book. Using various pseudonyms, writers like Gilbert Patten, Edward Stratemeyer, and John Wheeler created baseball-playing, All-American heroes like Frank Merriwell, Baseball Joe, and Lefty Locke to delight and instruct their juvenile audience. By the time Ring Lardner began to write the first modern baseball stories, the mythology of baseball was already in place. Dime novels and series books had valorized baseball as a combative yet democratic game, worthy of becoming America's national pastime because its heroes needed great skill, moral courage, and clear vision not only to make the perfect pitch or get the game-winning hit but to become successful members of American society. In early baseball fiction, a baseball hero also had to be a team player and a moral paragon, so that his achievement on the field and his rags-to-riches rise to fame validated baseball as the purest expression of the American Dream.

As a sports journalist, Ring Lardner knew better than to valorize baseball players as heroes or to celebrate the game as the American Dream. His baseball stories, from *You Know Me Al* to *Lose with a Smile*, debunk the traditional baseball narrative and deflate its pure-of-heart heroes. In his introduction to *You Know Me Al*, John Lardner claims that the Jack Keefe stories fix forever everything that is "inherently sound" and "characteristically silly" in baseball. He concludes that "all the essential truth about ball-playing can be found in *You Know Me Al* . . . there has never been a sounder baseball book." Even Holden Caufield, who finds phonies everywhere in *The Catcher in the Rye*, believes that Lardner's writing is the real thing.

Yet Lardner's stories, as authentic as they appear to be in their observation of ball playing, often perpetuate the view of baseball and ballplayers as larger than life because their narratives, like those of Shepard and Coover, tend to exploit even as they mock the high seriousness of baseball's mythology. Ring Lardner may have created the sound of an authentic American voice in *You Know Me Al* and *Lose with a Smile* by allowing Jack Keefe and Danny Warner to tell their own stories through the narrative ruse of letters to home, but the narratives of the letters are so incredible that Lardner in his own preface to *You Know Me Al* wrote that "no one with good sense" could possibly take the letters as being actual or real.

Jack Keefe and Danny Warner are talented ballplayers, but they clearly lack the moral qualities of the Great American Baseball Hero of the dime novels and serial books. Despite their own exaggerated claims to greatness, they fail because Lardner sends them up to his readers as manifestations of the Great American Boob. Each ballplayer, but Jack Keefe especially, rather than possessing heroic or even ordinary human qualities, exposes himself as ignorant and egotistical beyond belief. In *You Know Me Al*, Keefe damns himself by displaying no less than the Seven Deadly Sins before he falls to alcoholism and, in "The Busher Pulls a Mays," the last of the five additional Jack Keefe stories, is sold to the lowly Philadelphia Athletics. In Lardner's stories there is no salvation for Keefe because he commits the unforgivable sin of betraying his baseball talents; but at least for the reader there is the saving grace of Lardner's comic send-up of the worst faults of humanity, all puffed up and on display in a major-league baseball uniform: "Regards to all the boys and tell them I am still their pal and not all swelled up over this big league business."

Another widely recognized characteristic of Lardner's baseball stories, one that adds the appearance of substance to their sound of authenticity, is the use of real-life major-league players as foils to Lardner's fictitious bushers and boobs. Jack Keefe pitches in his well-filled White Sox uniform against the legendary Ty Cobb, Tris Speaker, and Babe Ruth, while coach Kid Gleason, fated to become manager of the 1919 Black Sox team, tries to put some sense into the busher's head, but to no effect: "'Well 1 of the waiters here in the hotel tells me a man can get all they want to drink here in Phila. if they go at it right but nothing doing Al as I am going to be in shape to give Gleason the best I got though 3 or 4 wouldn't hurt me and what Gleason don't know won't hurt him.'" In *Lose with a Smile*, Danny Warner, too raw to play a position, pinch hits against the likes of Wee Willie Sherdel, Jumbo Jim Elliot, Eppa Rixey, and Wild Bill Hallahan, while Brooklyn coach Casey Stengel alternatively ridicules and cajoles the thick-headed and thin-skinned rookie into paying attention to the fundamentals of the game: "'Stengel walked a long home with me and I ast him to come up and see my rm and he says ain't you going to eat nothing and I says I forgot all about it and he says that is what I thot when I seen you steal 3d base that you must of been out of your head all day and go and eat some thing and then write a letter to that little girl in Centralia because you certainly got enough to tell her tonight and I says she don't understand base ball and he says you ought to get a long fine.'"

This strategy of using real-life ballplayers in a fictional narrative, at least as old as Christy Mathewson's *Won in the Ninth*, a book Ring Lardner found corrupt, according to John Lardner, in its "observation of baseball procedures," gives Lardner's stories the sense and feel of baseball history; but, as John Lardner points out, "history, for the baseball-lover, is full of romance." While the narrative voice and the realistic details appear to give Lardner's baseball stories an air of reality, the inflated egos and outrageous behavior of Lardner's boobish narrators and the magical appeal of names like Cobb and Ruth also play to the view of baseball players as larger than life and the game itself as mythical. By freely mixing the historical, legendary, and fantastic, Lardner's stories actually blur the line between the credible and the incredible. As narrative models they anticipate the intertextuality of magic and realism now common to the baseball short story. As standards for baseball fiction they invite the celebration of baseball as a metaphor for American life and an expression of the American Dream even as they mock human nature.

Over the years, writers of baseball short stories have established a tradition for baseball fiction by creating delightful imitations of Ring Lardner's stories. Some, like James Thurber and Damon Runyon, have varied and even extended the imaginative possibilities of a Lardner narrative. In "You Could Look It Up," Thurber drops the historical pretensions of baseball fiction, facetiously recognized in the title, by narrating the story of something that "never'd come up in the history of the game before," at least to that point in baseball history. Thurber's tall tale of the first midget to play in a major-league baseball game delightfully displays the language of baseball as a sideshow of clichés— "See the armless pitchers, see the eyeless batters, see the infielders with five thumbs"—while it offers the wildest send-up of the conventional dramatics of the baseball narrative: "They ain't never been nothin' like it since creation was begun." Damon Runyon's "Baseball Hattie" has nothing in it to rival Thurber's climactic moment of a center fielder making a sensational game-ending catch of a flying midget, but Runyon's narrative, while less incredible, offers its own variation on Lardner. Runyon's "wonderful romance" between Baseball Hattie, "the worst bug of them all," and star pitcher Haystack Duggeler is also the story of the way a Lardnersque boob is saved from gamblers and his own incredible ignorance by his devoted wife. Her remedy is a bit severe and extreme even for baseball fiction, but Hattie, in shooting off her husband's pitching arm, saves the integrity of baseball, "the most honest game in all this world," and preserves her dream of her son pitching major-league baseball.

While Thurber and Runyon pay tribute to Lardner by extending and varying the screwball characters and unlikely adventures in his baseball stories, writers like Shepard and Coover have bent the Lardner narrative back upon itself and created baseball metafiction. Other writers, however, have soared beyond the exaggerated boundaries and parodies of Lardner's imitators and created a magical kingdom for baseball fiction. The most active exponent and practitioner of magical realism, W. P. Kinsella has created a world of fabulous and mythical happenings in his short stories. His readers encounter twins who form a baseball battery in their mother's womb, two ballplayers who transform themselves into a wolf and a great horned owl, and a team mascot who is actually an alien pretending that he's wearing a costume. In Kinsella's stories, Leo Durocher dines with J. D. Salinger and Bernard Malamud and has an opinion of *The Great Gatsby*; Christy Mathewson appears in the year 2000 to teach an honest manager how to throw the fadeaway; and Roberto Clemente, aged by only five days, floats to shore on a raft fifteen years after his death in a plane crash. Kinsella's stories also include a Chicago Cub manager who knows his team will finally win the pennant, but only on the day the world comes to a fiery end; a ballplayer who sells his soul for supernatural skills; and a fan who can trade his own life to resurrect the life of fallen Yankees star Thurman Munson, also tragically killed in a plane crash.

Kinsella's magical realm seems far removed from the sense and sound of Lardner's stories, as radically different in essence as shadow and substance. Kinsella's narrative strategies, however, are not that far removed from Lardner's in their execution of the baseball short story as the art of metaphor and hyperbole. Like Lardner and his imitators, Kinsella relies upon the voice of the storyteller to give his stories their credibility. As for character and plot, he also takes advantage of the gray area between history and legend and mixes fact and fantasy to create an entertaining fiction, but one envisioning baseball players as larger than life and the game as beyond the natural boundaries of time and space. Kinsella may have created a story in which an army of devoted fans painstakingly and secretively replace the artificial turf of a baseball stadium with real grass, but it's the thrill of the grass rather than what happens on real grass that most characterizes Kinsella's fiction.

Between Lardner's baseball yarns and Kinsella's magical tales, there have, of course, been short stories written in a fairly straightforward and seemingly realistic manner about the experiences of baseball. These stories look at baseball from multiple perspectives, ranging from the innocent eye of the child or the romantic vision of the devoted fan to the jaundiced view of the embittered ballplayer or the cynical observations of the hardened journalist. Their characters and plots range from the inexperienced but talented busher dreaming of his bright days to come in the major leagues to the embattled but crafty veteran trying to get through one more game or one more season in the sun before surrendering to the inevitable grayness of his career's end. Avoiding the trappings of the tall tale or the fairy tale, these stories tend to focus on tests of character within dramatic but conventional baseball situations.

The problem with the conventional baseball short story is that what passes for realism too easily slides into formulaic characters and plots and morally predictable and nostalgically sentimental outcomes. In anthologized stories from the 1940s and 1950s, like W. C. Heinz's "One Throw" and Arnold Hano's "The Umpire Was a Rookie," the green hero must either resist a Faustian temptation to compromise his great talent or overcome his failure to pass an earlier test of character. In stories like Stanley Frank's "Name of the Game" and Ashley Buck's "A Pitcher Grows Tired," the older hero must either defeat the selfishness and cynicism that threaten baseball, even at the sacrifice of his own career, or he must overcome the pain and exhaustion of age to continue playing the game he loves: "He wanted to play it forever—to pitch big-league ball until he died."

In other anthologized stories, gifted ballplayers betray their talents or fail to overcome their character flaws, but their failures often serve as moral lessons. In Robert Penn Warren's "Goodwood Comes Back," the narrator traces the doomed career and tragic death of an alcoholic pitcher who never adjusted from his country ways to the lonely city life of major-league baseball. Eliot Asinof's "The Rookie," a story that also serves as the concluding chapter of his novel, *Man on Spikes,* focuses on an aging ballplayer who fails at his chance to be a hero because of his declining skills and his inability to overcome his bitterness about the past. In J. F. Powers's "Jamesie," the narrator creates an interesting balance between a young boy's fantasies, fueled by his reading of the serialized adventures of "the courage and daring of Baseball Bill," and his devotion to Lefty, the star pitcher of the local team. The boy, however, learns a hard but valuable lesson about the risks of hero-worship when he discovers that Lefty is in with his gambling father and has thrown the big game.

When they are not spinning outrageous tales of Mahatma Gandhi pinch-hitting for Babe Ruth's Yankees or Fidel Castro pitching against two members of the 1951 Phillies or the first woman major-leaguer behaving worse than Ty Cobb and Ted Williams combined, contemporary writers have tried to give a harder edge to the baseball short story, but the conventions of baseball writing still show up in their narratives. In Andre Dubus's "The Pitcher," the green hero of gifted talents learns about his wife's infidelity and her decision to leave him just before the big game. Dubus's pitcher, however, shakes off the distraction of his personal life, pitches brilliantly, and, even though he loses the big game, recovers his history as a baseball player and his future as a major-league star at story's end. In Michael Chabon's "Smoke," a down-and-nearly-out pitcher attends the funeral of his former battery mate, a player of skill and intelligence, who was cut down in his prime in a car crash. Chabon's Max Magee is more antihero than aging hero, more stricken by his own demons than by the dishonesty of others; but even as he recognizes the absurdity of his life and his friend's death, he decides to continue his struggle to regain his pitching form and return to the big leagues. In the double narrative of Cris Mazza's "Caught," a former minor-league catcher struggles with the homosexual urges that have disrupted his passion for the rhythm of playing baseball and destroyed his baseball career. Caught between desire and loathing, Mazza's "bone bruiser" can only play out his emotional rage and his sexual frustration in a traditional game of catch, which nevertheless ends perversely and self-destructively when the ex-catcher deliberately takes a throw in his face.

In Jerry Klinkowitz's *Short Season*, the twenty-two baseball vignettes appear to avoid the conventions of baseball fiction by allowing a minor-league season to give the collection what Klinkowitz, in his introduction to *Writing Baseball*, has called its "integrity of structure." He also believes that his vignettes, by drawing their meaning from "the game's own phenomenology," have responded to the challenge of avoiding "the pontifications and easy invocations of humanistic ideals that spoil the game." Klinkowitz's comments have credibility in vignettes like "Ambience," where the narrative evokes its meaning from the special sounds of baseball. His claim that his stories avoid the conventions of baseball fiction does not, however, hold up well in a narrative populated by screwball characters playing out picaresque adventures or in the vignette that closes the collection with a no-hit championship game tossed by a home-team pitcher destined for the major leagues. In *Basepaths*, Klinkowitz's novelistic sequel to *Short Season*, the opening and closing stories are wonderful evocations of the magical connectedness of baseball and the potential loss of that connectedness through the mismanagement of the game; but the central narrative, like the vignettes in *Short Season*, plays out a series of improbable events within an absurd world plagued and eventually overrun by outlandish characters who drive a good-hearted and well-intentioned manager out of baseball only one week into the season.

Klinkowitz's observation in his introduction to the anthology *Writing Baseball* that baseball "is at once invented (as a game) and real (by virtue of its history and of its observable nature once underway)" appears to validate baseball fiction's tendencies toward the outlandish, the incredible, and the magical. It suggests that baseball generates its own characters and narratives, its own meaning and mythology, and baseball's writers merely provide delightful artifice where art already exists. In his introduction to the anthology *Baseball and the Game of Life*, Peter Bjarkman goes beyond this suggestion by stating that baseball, with its "distinctive personality types," its "carefully scripted roles," its "seasonal and daily cycles of play," and its "ever-expanding and theoretically unending time" is the very stuff of writers' dreams and their art of fiction.

The stories in the anthologies edited by Klinkowitz and Bjarkman certainly support the view that there are no apparent limits to characterization, narration, and resolution in the baseball short story. In highly implausible but morally instructive and nostalgically rendered tales, young boys learn valuable lessons about life while actually playing baseball alongside their childhood heroes. In separate stories a rookie with talent at the level of great art walks into the narrative "straight out of Ring Lardner," while an aging pitcher rediscovers his love for "that simplest of actions, that purity of motion, throwing a ball back and forth" at the same time as he rejects the business and politics of the professional game. There are spoofs of baseball rhetoric and the exaggerated storytelling of oral histories, a politically edged satire of Fidel Castro's fanaticism for baseball and revolution, and even tales from the twilight zone about a player giving miraculous birth to baseballs and a reporter almost losing his soul for Ted Williams–like eyes.

In *Diamonds Are a Girl's Best Friend*, Elinor Nauen's anthology of women writers on baseball, the baseball short stories, ranging from Edna Ferber's "A Bush League Hero" and S. W. M. Humason's "Madame Southpaw" to Roberta Israeloff's "City Ball," Oona Short's "The Truth about Paradise," and Patricia Highsmith's "The Barbarians," show the same tendency to serve up extravagant or contrived narratives with unlikely or ridiculous characters and improbable or outrageous plots. Their narratives either exaggerate baseball stereotypes for comic effect or manipulate the field of play to suit some morally instructive conclusion about the best and the worst of human nature. Whether the central character is a troubled young girl learning something about failed dreams and dreams recaptured by going to her first game with her grandfather, or a gullible young woman discovering that her "blond god standing on the pitcher's mound" fails to shine as brightly in his off-season job as a shoe clerk, or a fanatical crone-like woman who reminds Roger Paradise, "the epitome of baseball," that "he loved baseball so damn much," the short stories in *Diamonds Are a Girl's Best Friend* are a perfect fit within the traditional narratives of baseball fiction.

What often seems absent in baseball's short stories is a consideration of baseball as an ordinary event on an ordinary day—not all games are the final or seventh game—or an interest in turning the ordinary, the common, and the routine in baseball into the extraordinary through a narrative art limited by an air of reality or the ring of truth, rather than inflated by the traditional belief in the generative and transformative power of the game itself. Lacking the tradition of realism in the modern short story, baseball's stories, with their sound of the tall tale and their aura of fable, legend, and myth, have taken readers through fiction's looking glass but have seldom allowed a reflective and realistic look at the looking glass's nicely polished surface.

Once through the looking glass, baseball's readers do encounter a wonderland of fantastic characters and adventures to rival the imaginative world of Lewis Carroll. They can watch the screwball antics of Zane Grey's redheaded outfielder or follow Grey's innocent and gullible Rube on his journey to the major leagues. They are as likely to encounter the ridiculous in a horse named Jones playing third base for Brooklyn and a gorilla named the Great McWhiff pitching against Joe DiMaggio as they are to witness the sublime in Frank O'Rourke's heavenly World Series between American and National League immortals. They can read incredible letters written by illiterate bushers and boobs or listen in on Faustian offers of supernatural baseball skills. They can even turn to the shifting and uncertain world of the contemporary short story and still find the mysterious in Stuart Dybek's right fielder dying young; the nostalgic if not miraculous in Ethan Canin's Red Sox fan who solves his midlife crisis when he takes his adult son to a baseball game at Fenway Park; and the magical and timeless in T. Coraghessan Boyle's aging ballplayer of ordinary skills who still believes, as does Boyle and so many writers and readers of baseball fiction, in the heroic and mythical possibilities of baseball:

> This is the game that never ends. When the heavy hitters have fanned and the pitchers' arms gone sore, when there's no joy in Mudville, taxes are killing everybody, and the Russians are raising hell in Guatemala, when the manager paces the dugout like an attack dog, mind racing, searching high and low for the canny veteran to go in and do single combat, there he'll be—always, always eternal as a monument—Hector Quesadilla, utility infielder, with the .296 lifetime average and service with the Reds, Phils, Cubs, Royals, and L.A. Dodgers.

In Don DeLillo's "Pafko at the Wall," the narrative manipulates the circumstances surrounding an historic baseball moment too sacred in itself to be altered or tampered with even by baseball fiction. Bobby Thomson's famous home run has yet to curve foul in baseball fiction, but in DeLillo's story, just as Ralph Branca delivers his fateful pitch, Jackie Gleason, after a gargantuan bout of eating and drinking, vomits all over Leo Durocher's choice box at the Polo Grounds and all over the socks and shoes of Frank Sinatra. Of course, in the magical world of baseball fiction Bobby Thomson would never have had the opportunity to time his historic swing with Gleason's stream of vomit had not the young-boy-turned-major-league hitter in Kinsella's "How I Got My Nickname" tripped the pinch hitter Durocher had decided to send up to bat for Thomson, thereby preserving baseball history and earning the kid his nickname, "The Tripper."

◆7◆
Naturals and Supernaturals: Baseball Fiction's Long Game

In "Horatio at the Bat; or, Why Such a Lengthy Embryonic Period for the Serious Baseball Novel," Mark Harris briefly summarizes what has now become the standard view of the history of the baseball novel. With no tradition beyond the moral romances and rags-to-riches stories of the dime novels and series books, the baseball novel stayed, for the most part, at the level of juvenile fiction until the 1950s. With no Ring Lardner to offer a comic counternarrative to the sentimental tradition of the Horatio Alger story and with the popularity of the juvenile novels of John Tunis in the 1940s, the serious baseball novel did not begin its development until the *annus mirabilis* of 1952 and the publication of Bernard Malamud's *The Natural*, followed a year later by Harris's *The Southpaw*.

For Harris, the appearance of his own novel marked the end of the tradition of sentimentality and the beginning of "the realistic tradition of the baseball novel." *The Natural*, however, angered Harris because "Malamud just wasn't realistic baseball." Rather than pioneering realism in the baseball novel, *The Natural* encouraged baseball readers to believe that for baseball to be treated seriously as a literary topic it had to be symbolic and mythic. Eventually, Harris, prompted by the publication of Philip Roth's outrageously satirical *Great American Novel* in 1973, decided that what he and Malamud had done twenty years earlier, despite their radically different approaches, was to liberate artists and critics to write seriously about baseball. With the Baseball Joe of juvenile fiction banished to biography, the Horatio Alger tradition was now replaced in the serious novel by "fantasy sometimes, realism sometimes, problem solving, ventures into myth, symbolism, baseball futurism, baseball science-fiction, into the very homosexuality for which Horatio Alger was condemned and fired from his ministry only 125 years earlier, drugs and other illegal or shadowy activities which make the alleged thievery of Baseball Joe seem tame indeed."

Harris's narrative of the emergence of the serious baseball novel is the stuff of fiction itself and, actually, the stuff of Harris's own fiction as well. For Harris, the baseball novel, like the Henry Wiggen of the Harris tetralogy, has trouble growing up, eventually reaches maturation after learning something about tolerance and responsibility, and finally comes to recognize and accept human frailty and failure as contextual with baseball itself. Harris's narrative is also compatible with the traditional view of American literature as the story of Huckleberry Finn and Holden Caufield, of America's youth struggling to preserve its innocence against the harsh realities of adulthood until it can find some meaningful identity and role in a rapidly changing and developing American society. If placed within the narrative context of Harris's story of the maturation of the baseball novel, Huck, of course, can now grow up to be a baseball writer and convert his journey down the Mississippi into mythical and magical tales about baseball, while Holden, a great admirer of Ring Lardner, can write comic but realistic baseball novels that tell the truth about American society and the human condition.

The story of the serious baseball novel as a neatly divided stream flowing in one direction from *The Natural* into the imaginative world of metafiction and magic realism and in the opposite direction from *The Southpaw* into the realistic world of adult problems and contemporary controversies has, like Lardner's short stories, a nice sound to it and perhaps even the ring of truth. The truthfulness of its vision, however, is dependent upon Harris's assumptions about the mythic and symbolic nature of *The Natural* and the realistic and frank nature of *The Southpaw*. To accept Harris's view of the serious baseball novel is to see *The Natural* as the epitome of the narrative transformation of baseball into magic and myth and *The Southpaw* as the end of the Horatio Alger tradition in baseball and the beginning of a tradition of realism.

The critical reaction, over the years, to *The Natural* and *The Southpaw* appears to support Harris's claims for the two novels. Ever since Earl Wasserman's Jungian interpretation of *The Natural* as Malamud's "World Ceres," critics, supported by Malamud's own statement that he "wasn't able to write about the game until [he] transformed game into myth," have searched for magical symbols and rituals with the same zeal and cunning as Joyceans in excavating the mythic landscape of *Ulysses*. As for *The Southpaw* and Harris's other baseball novels, they are routinely praised for their Lardnersque ability to capture the sights and sounds of baseball, while creating realistic characters who, according to Donald Hall, play out, against the exciting and compelling background of baseball action, "their moral quotidian dramas."

The persistent and successful search for mythic and symbolic meaning in *The Natural* and the elevation of the novel's characters and action to the mystical and cosmic has actually taken its lead from Malamud, who claimed he was able to transform baseball into myth, "via Jessie Weston's Percival legend with an assist by T. S. Eliot's 'The Waste Land' plus the lives of several ballplayers I had read, in particular Babe Ruth's and Bobby Feller's. The myth enriched the baseball lore as feats of magic transformed the game." By drawing attention to Jessie Weston's *From Ritual to Romance* and T. S. Eliot's *The Waste Land*, works heavily dependent upon J. G. Frazer's monumental *The Golden Bough* for their own symbolic meaning and mythic scaffolding,

Malamud invites a reading of *The Natural* as a narrative blend of ancient vegetation myths of wounded heroes and blighted lands and the romantic legends of the knightly quest for the Holy Grail. By also evoking baseball's own legendary heroes and feats, Malamud makes the invitation to a mythic or romantic reading even more enticing by offering serious baseball readers the irresistible proposition that baseball has the same magical, moral, and spiritual potency of ancient religious rituals and transformative religious journeys.

From the perspective of mythic romance, *The Natural* becomes the storied adventure of baseball's wounded hero-scapegoat, a flawed Lancelot of extraordinary physical skills waving his talismanic Wonderboy at enemy pitchers in a failed but epic effort to rescue the jinxed and aging Pop Fisher and his ineffectual and spiritless New York Knights from a baseball wasteland corrupted and controlled by evil ownership. Instead of struggling against the wild beasts, chthonian gods, and murderous priests of Frazer's *Golden Bough*, Roy Hobbs encounters figures from baseball's own legendary past: egotistical baseball heroes and murderous groupies, the sinister gambler and the insidious sportswriter, and, above all, the greedy and manipulative owner. Rather than finding salvation in Frazer's Sacred Marriage or in Weston's quest for the Holy Grail, Malamud's natural can seek out his redemption within the history of the game itself by hitting the pennant-winning home run—"Only a homer, with himself scoring the winning run, would truly redeem him"—and becoming the greatest player of all time: "Sometimes when I walk the street I bet people will say there goes Roy Hobbs, the best there ever was in the game."

While constructing a mythic scaffolding that makes *The Natural* one of the most literary-minded baseball novels of all time, Malamud develops a narrative that also relies on the capacity of baseball to generate its own stories of mythic heroes, fools, and villains, of fabled adventures and episodes, and of legendary confrontations and climaxes. Just as the literary reader of *The Natural* can gather up the narrative allusions to the ancient stories of Adonis, Attis, and Osiris and the medieval romances of Arthur, Lancelot, and Galahad, the baseball reader of Malamud's novel can find narrative fragments from the legends of Ruth, Feller, and Stengel, as well as from a series of baseball misadventures and tragedies, including the shooting of Eddie Waitkus, the wall crashing of Pete Reiser, and the bribery of Joe Jackson. And just as the ancient and medieval storyteller needed to convert mythic heroes into religious scapegoats to ensure, in their sacrifice, the coming of a new season and the regeneration of the land and the spirit of the people, the modern reader, taking the lead from Malamud, can find in Roy Hobbs and his failure to hit the game-winning home run the archetype of the baseball hero as scapegoat or victim dating back to the historical Joe Jackson and the literary Mighty Casey, heroes who brought no joy to Mudville but continue to fascinate, delight, and awe baseball fans, while validating their faith in the baseball adage "wait until next year"—even though T. S. Eliot, in *The Waste Land,* did warn baseball fans and literary scholars like A. Bartlett Giamatti that even April can be the cruelest month.

This symbolic reading of *The Natural* as the happy narrative wedding of the myths and fables of ancient and medieval hero-scapegoats and the legends of once-mighty-but-now-fallen baseball heroes also anticipates the standard readings of Robert Coover's *Universal Baseball Association, Inc., J. Henry Waugh, Prop.* and Philip Roth's *Great American Novel* as the worthy successors to Malamud's symbolic and mythic novel. In *The Universal Baseball Association,* however, the narrative shifts from a symbolic reading of baseball's own legendary past to the phantasmagoric rendering of the fabricated history of a baseball dice league. In Coover's novel, the narrative perspective also shifts from the baseball hero obsessed with his own immortality to the baseball fan in love not with "the actual game so much—to tell the truth real baseball bored him—but rather the records, the statistics, the peculiar balances between individual and team, offense and defense, strategy and luck, accident and pattern, power and intelligence. And no other activity in the world had so precise and comprehensive a history, so specific an ethic, and at the same time, strange as it seemed, so much ultimate mystery."

In J. Henry Waugh, Coover has created the perfect narrative counterpart to Malamud's Roy Hobbs. Instead of encountering the baseball phenom or wounded hero who wants to live forever through his baseball statistics, the reader encounters the lonely and isolated baseball fan who compensates for his boring and dismal life by inventing a dice league and living vicariously through its statistics and history. When the historical and ethical balance of Waugh's dice league is shattered and turned into a spiritual wasteland by one horrifying roll of the dice and the fatal beaning of wunderkind Damon Rutherford, Waugh can recover from his dark night of the soul only when he elevates the Universal Baseball Association from invented or fabled history to mythic or religious allegory through the transformative power of a ritual beaning enacted on Damonsday each season. At first in love with baseball records, Coover's manic accountant discovers in the mysterious authority of rituals and in the redemptive power of baseball that "perfection wasn't a thing, a closed moment, a static fact, but *process,* yes, and the process was transformation."

In *The Great American Novel,* Philip Roth completes the trinity of baseball's great symbolic novels by adding the madly alliterative baseball writer, Word Smith, to Malamud's hero-scapegoat and Coover's messianic fan. The Gargantua of baseball narratives, Roth's novel also serves up baseball's most incredible lineup of misfits, its most outrageous team performance, and its most improbable or fantastic plot. Roth's 1943 Port Ruppert Mundys, the Pequod of baseball teams, is a compendium of oddities from baseball fact and fiction. The players range in age from fourteen to fifty-two, in personality from innocent phenom to ex-convict, "the bastard off-spring of the only pitcher ever to dare to throw a pissball in a major-league ball park," and in appearance from a one-legged catcher and a one-armed outfielder to a relief pitcher with an arm so sore he rolls his warm-up pitches to the catcher. The Mundys' most dramatic win comes in an exhibition game against the inmates of an insane asylum, but the joy is short-lived when a midget pitches a shutout against them in their next major-league game. The team's season record of 34-120 is punctuated by a record season-ending 31-0 loss in a game attended by Judge Kenesaw Mountain Landis and Eleanor Roosevelt. As for plot, *The Great American Novel* is a surreal tale full of sound and fury told by a sportswriter gone mad about the attempt of Gil Gamesh, a banned baseball pitcher turned Russian agent, to use the Mundys as dupes in a Communist conspiracy against the great American institution of baseball. Though Gamesh fails to destroy the national game, his plotting leads to the banishment of the Mundy Thirteen, the dismantling of the Mundy team, the purge of all its team records, and finally the elimination of the misnamed Patriot League from baseball history.

In the process of adding the obsessed and delusional sportswriter to Malamud's wounded and flawed natural and Coover's lonely fan turned religious fanatic, Roth brings the mythic and symbolic novel full cycle by turning its narrative completely back upon itself. In Word Smith's Ahab-like pursuit of the Great American Novel, Roth's narrative, while reaching the nethermost region of satirical rage and subversive parody, draws attention to the misguided and dangerous tendency of old-time baseball players in their myriad oral histories to romanticize the history of the game, of baseball's most devoted and ardent fans to transform the statistical records of the playing of the game into a sacred text, and of baseball's most serious writers to envision symbolic meaning and mythic ritual in baseball, while failing to see it as social history and its participants as psychologically interesting human beings. Viewed from the perspective of Roth's ultimate parody of the serious baseball narrative, Malamud's *The Natural* and Coover's *Universal Baseball Association,* as well as Roth's own novel, succeed only to the degree to which they use the symbolic, mythic, and transformative tendencies of baseball's traditional narratives as an ironic or parodic strategy to draw out some significant or at least interesting aspect of the social or human fabric of baseball rather than merely supporting the claim for baseball as the mystic repository of some universal meaning or timeless lesson for its players, fans, and writers.

The ultimate irony of the mythic and symbolic baseball novels of Malamud, Coover, and Roth is that their success with readers is greatly dependent upon the same stylistic extravagance and narrative exaggeration that damn Word Smith's manuscript to a writer's limbo of eternal rejection notices. Rarely rejected and often praised by baseball's readers, *The Natural, The Universal Baseball Association,* and *The Great American Novel,* while deeply insightful in their criticism of baseball's traditional tendencies toward hero worshipping, mythmaking, and historical distortion, have earned their place in the history of the baseball novel by taking advantage of the same stilted stylistic and narrative strategies that have raised the game of baseball to the lofty and sometimes dizzying heights of romance, legend, and myth. Like the short stories of Lardner, the baseball novels of Malamud, Coover, and Roth are narrative paradoxes, freely mixing fact and fancy, readily describing the extraordinary as the ordinary, and routinely transforming the human condition into the supernatural, metaphysical, or fantastical.

The legacy of the mythic and symbolic narratives of Malamud, Coover, and Roth is evident in the now common appearance of exaggerated characters, exotic settings, improbable if not ludicrous plots, outrageous coincidences, and contrived endings in baseball novels. In baseball's galaxy of fiction, Malamud's New York Knights, Coover's Damonites and Caseyites, and Roth's Ruppert Mundys have been joined by the Dead Knights of Nancy Willard's *Things Invisible to See,* the redeemed and resurrected Immortals of Kinsella's *Shoeless Joe,* and the Freudian misfits of David Carkeet's *The Greatest Slump of All Time.* Baseball fiction's larger-than-life heroes now include the exiled but indomitable Babe Ragland, the "bossman-magician" of Jerome Charyn's *The Seventh Babe;* the defiant and homicidal Mason Tidewater, the "Black Babe" of Negro baseball and the homosexual lover of baseball's own Babe Ruth, in Jay Neugeboren's *Sam's Legacy;* and the Zen Buddhist pitching phenom with the 160-mile-per-hour fast-ball of George Plimpton's *The Curious Case of Sidd Finch*. As for plot, readers of Kinsella's *Iowa Baseball Confederacy* can walk through a crack in time in Iowa and watch a July 4, 1908, exhibition game be-tween the world-champion Chicago Cubs and an all-star team from a mythical baseball league, or in Darryl Brock's *If I Never Get Back* they can get off an Amtrak train in Ohio and join up with the 1869 Cincinnati Red Stockings, baseball's first professional team. When not time traveling, readers can barnstorm through America with Babe Ragland's Cincinnati Colored Giants and its cast of baseball outcasts and oddities, including its own witch doctor, or take up with the Brook-lyn Bimbos of John Sayles's *Pride of the Bimbos,* a five-man fast-pitch softball team that plays in women's clothing and features a dwarf positioned (where else?) at shortstop.

If Joe Jackson walking out of an Iowa field of corn is not magic enough for baseball's readers, in Gordon Alpine's *Joy in Mudville* they can follow a glowing baseball, which turns out to be a prodigious home run hit by Babe Ruth, traveling from Chicago to the West Coast. If Ray Kinsella playing catch with the conjured ghost of his dead father is not enough sentiment for baseball's readers, in John Alexander Graham's *Babe Ruth Caught in a Snowstorm* they can indulge their love of the game by following the gullible and unbelievable Wichita Wraiths, an amateurish and oddball team of players who qualify for the team solely on the basis of their desire to play baseball. If base-ball's readers prefer a touch of the bizarre with their baseball fanta-sies, they will find in Tony Ardizzone's *Heart of the Order* a major-league player who believes he is possessed by the spirit of a childhood friend he killed with a line drive or discover in James McManus's *Chin Music* a beaned major-league pitcher who wakes out of a coma and wanders home for a last-minute reconciliation with his son on the day of an approaching nuclear apocalypse. If baseball's readers become nostalgic for the politically absurd and outrageous, they can simply follow in Donald Hays's *The Dixie Association* the adventures of the

Arkansas Reds, a subversive team of misfits made up of a former con-
vict, who also serves as narrator, and a militant assortment of Chero-
kees, Communists, and Castro Cubans, along with a Black Muslim
and the first woman to appear in professional baseball, all led by a left-
wing, one-armed manager. Considering all the fantastical goings on
in the mythic and symbolic baseball novel, Leonard Everett Fisher's
author's note to *Noonan: A Novel about Baseball, ESP, and Time
Warps* seems to state the obvious in the symbolic novel rather than
offer some warning or revelation to his reader: "The story you are
about to read is ridiculous. It never happened. . . . Most of the leading characters you will meet are absolutely fictitious. I invented
them. . . . In the interest of the narrative, the appearance, behavior, and
conversation of . . . real personages bear little resemblance to actual-
ity—their nature, deeds and legends. Should these matters bear such
resemblance, it would not only be coincidental, it would be a shocking revelation."

The alternative to or perhaps the antidote for the sublime-to-the-
ridiculous narratives of mythic and symbolic baseball novels, at least
according to Mark Harris, is the realistic narrative of novels that are
actually about baseball. Generally regarded as entertaining and successful attempts to capture the voice, rhythm, and color of baseball,
Harris's own tetralogy of baseball novels appears to offer baseball's
readers this antidote, while also validating Harris's claim that his novels
have provided the narrative prototype as well as the structural foundation for a tradition of realism to counter all the mythic scaffolding
and symbol making in the baseball novel. Harris's novels are so given
to creating a realistic narrative about baseball that they include official rosters, special souvenir programs, and detailed accounts of games.
They also provide a narrator/ballplayer who, after growing up on a
steady diet of baseball stories by "Sherman and Heyliger and Tunis
and Lardner," decides to write a truthful book about baseball in reaction to the self-serving cynicism and sensationalism of tabloid journalism and the "usual slop" of baseball entertainments "where nobody

sweats and nobody swears and every game is crucial and the stands are always packed and the clubhouse always neat as a pin and the women always beautiful and the manager always tough on the outside with a tender heart of gold beneath and everybody either hits the first pitch or fans on 3."

Told in the first person by Henry Wiggen, a gifted pitcher for the New York Mammoths, Harris's *The Southpaw, Bang the Drum Slowly, A Ticket for a Seamstitch*, and *It Looked Like Forever* chronicle Wiggen's entire baseball career from its beginnings, highlighted by a sensational rookie season, through his early struggles and eventual recovery of his Hall of Fame form, to his pursuit of baseball immortality and his fateful and nearly fatal last pitch. *The Southpaw,* its narrative a strong expression of Wiggen's love of playing baseball is, like *The Adventures of Huckleberry Finn* and *The Catcher in the Rye,* a coming-of-age novel. At novel's end, Wiggen's future wife tells him that he had a successful first year in the major leagues not because of his statistics, awards, or the Mammoths championship but because he overcame his moral mistakes and his errors of judgment, learned something about human nature and his own character, and "growed to manhood over the summer." In *Bang the Drum Slowly,* the narrative shifts from youthful awakening to more manly concerns and responsibilities as Wiggen, now more Nick Carraway than Huck Finn, learns from a dying teammate with far less talent and intelligence something about the value of team camaraderie and personal loyalty and friendship. Disappointed in himself for failing to honor his teammate's last request, a scorecard from the Mammoths' World Series victory, Wiggen recovers his moral balance by becoming a pallbearer at Bruce Pearson's funeral and offering the reader an appropriate epitaph as well as a lesson in human conduct: "He was not a bad fellow, no worse than most and probably better than some, and not a bad ballplayer neither when they give him a chance, when they laid off him long enough. From here on in I rag nobody."

Though easily the slightest in content, the most comic in intention, and the shortest in length of Harris's baseball novels, *A Ticket for a Seamstitch* continues the moral education of Henry Wiggen, this time through the adoring loyalty and fierce determination of a female fan willing to travel across the continent at the risk of her safety and virtue to meet her idol and see the Mammoths play on the Fourth of July. While the novel, despite its pretentious preface, serves, at best, as a comic interlude after all the tragic seriousness of *Bang the Drum Slowly*, its narrative events do teach Wiggen something about the attractiveness of resiliency and decency even in the most ordinary-looking of human beings, while Wiggen also learns an important lesson about the elusiveness and fickleness of baseball fame and fortune. In *It Looked Like Forever*, the last novel in Harris's tetralogy, Henry Wiggen has his fame and at least a modest fortune, but now he has to face up to his advancing age, declining skills, and a life without baseball. After a period of avoidance and a brief comeback as a relief pitcher for the Mammoths' chief rival, Wiggen finally decides to end his career, though it takes a line drive to the head for him to accept his failing instincts. Once he goes through the painful therapy of watching the cassette of his last pitch, he acknowledges that he "was no longer a baseball player and had not been a baseball player since the eighth inning Friday in California. . . . After a while I no longer required the film but give it to the Hall of Fame at Cooperstown N.Y., along with many other silvernears from time gone by."

In *It Looked Like Forever*, Henry Wiggen reads what turns out to be a premature retirement notice in which he is described as a sometime author who "stimulated interest in baseball among readers who had never suspected its human dimension." Except for the "sometime," the notice appears to be an apt description of Mark Harris's vision of his baseball novels as the vanguard of a tradition of realism. Yet, as impressive as Harris's novels are in capturing the vernacular of baseball and the career struggles of the baseball hero, the narratives still rely upon typical baseball characters, including a baseball natural who learns his love of the game from his father, and upon conventional strategies of fiction writing. As baseball entertainments, the novels take full advantage of the formulaic narrative of a baseball player of extraordinary talent playing out his personal conflicts and moral dilemmas within the high drama of tight pennant races and record-breaking performances. As literary events, the novels use baseball, despite Harris's claim in his preface to *A Ticket for a Seamstitch* that as a storyteller he leaves "morality in the other room," as the setting for moral romances or fables about the lessons of growing up, the value of love, and finally the acceptance of growing old. Henry Wiggen, throughout the tetralogy, remains interesting as a baseball player, but he hardly evolves into an interesting human being capable of recognizing reality and acting maturely unless, of course, reality smacks him in the head with a line drive.

The problem for Harris, as he recognized in his essay on the serious baseball novel, is that his novels, while realistic in detail and event, owe a great debt to the sentimental narratives of the Horatio Alger tradition. In "Bring Back That Old Sandlot Novel," Harris acknowledges that "my boy Henry Wiggen *does* succeed, *does* grow rich, *does* protect and preserve his moral virtue." The result is a series of baseball novels with the trappings of realism that nevertheless remain sentimental and superficial as literary narratives. While they appear to offer a realistic look at baseball, Harris's novels hardly mark the beginning of a tradition of realism for baseball's readers. Instead they open the door for baseball novels that often display a surface or superficial realism but rarely advance beyond baseball stereotypes and hackneyed plotting. Stripped of their realistic appearance, these novels, even when dealing with radical or controversial subjects, often reveal themselves in substance and intention as the emotionally sentimental and morally instructive descendants of the Horatio Alger tradition of baseball writing rather than as the worthy heirs of a tradition of realism.

The most obvious and the most serious problem in what passes for realistic baseball novels is their addiction to formulaic narratives. Like their baseball short-story counterparts, they rely heavily upon conventional baseball characters and situations and morally or emotionally predictable resolutions or outcomes. Their narratives are usually about the physical and emotional demands of playing baseball and the inevitable moral crisis that always seems to materialize in the seventh game of the World Series or its equivalent. Their moment of truth or narrative epiphanies come with the last perfect pitch thrown, the last graceful swing of the bat, or the last great catch. In the typical coming-of-age novel, like Ed Fitzgerald's formulaic *The Ballplayer,* the narrative follows the trials and tryouts of a youth consumed by the dream of playing major-league baseball. Inevitably the youth overcomes life's obstacles and baseball's hardships and, proving virtue and hard work are rewarded, becomes not only a big-league player but "the hero of all the heroes." In the conventional novel about the aging and fading baseball veteran, like Roger Kahn's *The Seventh Game,* the narrative, since it focuses on the end of a baseball career, usually fuses the veteran's emotional conflicts and moral dilemmas with the playing of his final game. And even if the narrative adds the ironic twist of the veteran losing his final game and his last chance at a championship season, his determined performance reveals a courage that will help him make the right decisions about the rest of his life: "Final score don't mean nothing. . . . I'm here to shake hands with a winning pitcher."

The narrative formula of baseball as a moral and emotional testing ground also routinely appears in novels about those excluded, shunned, or exiled from baseball's history and traditions. John Hough Jr.'s *The Conduct of the Game,* for example, takes up the taboo subject of homosexuality in baseball, but the novel relies heavily upon the conventional coming-of-age narrative. In Hough's novel, Lee Malcolm, a talented rookie umpire in love with baseball and devoted to his profession, learns, like the Henry Wiggen of *Bang the Drum Slowly,* something about the value of camaraderie and friendship, in this case from a homosexual rather than a fatally ill roommate. Malcolm actually gives up his career after his friend commits suicide because he has learned that the conduct of his life is more important than the conduct of the game. In Barbara Gregorich's *She's on First,* Linda Sunshine, the first female to play major-league baseball, is able to overcome prejudice and abuse by learning from her sportswriter lover that she is special only because baseball players and the game itself are special. Rather than giving up her career, she, like fictional heroes from Baseball Joe to Highpockets, learns that the game and the team are more important than individual pride: "When you get a bad pitch—even a pitch that knocks you off your feet and into the backstop—you get up and take the base you earned."

The narrative of *She's on First* is emotionally contrived and cliché-driven and its game descriptions are sometimes flawed and muddled, but Gregorich's novel gains some strength and credibility from its attempt to place the struggles of Linda Sunshine within the historical context of the ill-fated All-American Girls Professional Baseball League. This strategy is similar to William Brashler's use of the history of Negro League professional baseball in *The Bingo Long Traveling All-Stars and Motor Kings.* While Brashler's novel is vulnerable to the criticism that its narrative distorts reality because it relies too much on comic descriptions of baseball clowning, it is far more comprehensive and effective in its treatment of discrimination than *She's on First.* Despite its sentimental bow to Jackie Robinson's crossing of the color line at novel's end, Brashler's novel does show the possibility of countering the tendency of baseball novels toward moral romance and romantic tragedy by grounding character and plot in baseball history.

In Harry Stein's *Hoopla* and Brendan Boyd's *Blue Ruin,* both historical novels about the Black Sox scandal, the narratives avoid romantic stereotyping and facile moral tags by looking at the scandal from the more complex perspective of the cultural expectations and social realities of the time. *Hoopla,* for example, develops its narrative from the double perspective of Buck Weaver's determination to tell what really happened—"maybe it's time some individual set down the actual truth for a change"—and the yellow journalism and moral relativism of baseball columnist Luther Pond: "'If a man is popular Pond, you bring him down a notch, don't you. . . . And if a man is in desperate straits you force the reader to care about him.'" While Weaver's inside account exposes the desperate conditions that drove the players into fixing the World Series, Pond's columns offer up the scandal as "the harbinger of an approaching age" of moral duplicity and self-serving individualism. In *Blue Ruin* the narrative takes a more subterranean and subversive look at the Black Sox scandal by offering its readers the cynical perspective of a minor-league hood: "There is no truth, only versions." Sport Sullivan's version of the truth is that he set the fix in motion because he too had a dream, in this case the perverted dream of becoming a big-league gangster like Arnold Rothstein: "a man of undisputed powers with unexpected limitations, a heightened version of myself, perhaps; and as I would have him—a man who keeps to himself, a man who makes things work, a man who knows."

There are also baseball novellas or novels, like Don DeLillo's "Pafko at the Wall," that self-consciously frame their narratives within periods of critical social or political changes in America or, like Mark Winegardner's *The Veracruz Blues,* create a revisionist history to counter a codified period in baseball history or to recover a lost or obscured historical event. "Pafko at the Wall," for example, witnesses Bobby Thomson's now immortalized home run from the unsettling perspective of America's neurotic cultural, political, and racial attitudes of the early fifties. While Russ Hodges makes his legendary call, J. Edgar Hoover, Jackie Gleason, and Frank Sinatra, representatives of the fifties' dark age of politics and its gluttonous age of entertainment, look on from Leo Durocher's private box. As Thomson circles the bases, a black youth from the ghetto and a white middle-class male struggle for possession of the home-run ball.

In *The Veracruz Blues,* the obscure misadventure of the Mexican League's raid on the American major leagues, now revised, becomes the historical precursor to the unionization of baseball and the elimination of the reserve clause as well as a reminder of the historical exclusion of black ballplayers from baseball and its traditional narratives. Told from multiple perspectives, ranging from "the youngest and most lost member of the Lost Generation," who, like Roth's Word Smith, has dreamt of writing the Great American Novel, to a proud and bitter Negro League star pitcher who dreamt of being the first black player to cross baseball's color line, Winegardner's novel transforms a minor incident in baseball history into "one of the great adventures in baseball history." It also converts a cast of misfits, malcontents, and egomaniacs into misbegotten and exiled heroes perfect for a postmodern narrative "rich with masks, poses, irony, and paradox," if not suitable for baseball's dream narrative.

The use of subversive or multiple perspectives has worked well in baseball's historical novels, but it is also used as an effective strategy in Eliot Asinof's *Man on Spikes,* a realistic novel published two years after Harris's *The Southpaw,* which tells the story of a ballplayer who struggles for sixteen years before finally appearing in a major-league game, only to fail in his moment of truth. Even though Asinof's novel has often been overlooked by critics in their search for the serious baseball novel, *Man on Spikes* is a remarkably balanced and intimate study of the various forces at play in the life and career of a baseball player. Avoiding, for the most part, the baseball stereotypes, the contrived dramatic heroics, and the emotional sentiments and moral simplifications that often plague the realistic baseball novel, Asinof's narrative uses fourteen different perspectives, beginning with the baseball scout and concluding with the ballplayer's own point of view, to create a detailed and comprehensive portrait of Mike Kutner, a player of great abilities, not because he is a baseball natural but because he loves baseball well enough to play the game well: "The kid was young, say nineteen or so, but he looked like he'd been playing scientific baseball all his life."

Opening in the 1930s, Asinof's narrative uses the perspective of the old-time baseball scout to establish the contrast between the smart and aggressive play of the dead-ball era and the current live-ball era of the

Ruthian home run: "It's the goddamn long ball they want now. . . . That's baseball today. It just ain't a little man's game." Within this historical context, Asinof introduces his protagonist, a short, slight, bespectacled center fielder who is no Roy Hobbs or Henry Wiggen in stature but in his instincts, determination, and grace seems, at least from the perspective of the old-time scout, to have the real talent and intelligence to play major-league baseball. Once Asinof's narrative establishes the skilled and dedicated baseball character of his man on spikes and places him within the arbitrary and irrational demands of the time for more Babe Ruths and less Ty Cobbs, the novel, through its shifting perspectives, follows Kutner through a series of personal crises and professional ordeals that undermine baseball's dream narrative with its fathers playing catch with sons and its immortalized baseball heroes playing on timeless and endless fields of dreams. Instead of a romantic vision of baseball, Asinof's narrative offers baseball's readers a sharply focused, uncompromising view of the short-sightedness and the narrow-mindedness, the petty jealousies and arbitrary judgments that are at the heart of professional baseball.

In *Man on Spikes* readers encounter a Depression-era father who has no interest in baseball or playing catch with his son—"These were the 1930's, and playing was for the rich"—and a mean-spirited, manipulative manager without the conventional heart of gold. Instead of moral lessons about the conduct of the game, readers learn from a washed-up veteran that "baseball is a game of personalities, like any other business" and from a baseball trickster that fans enjoy and love their baseball clowns more than the game's serious performers. Rather than finding virtue and hard work rewarded, readers see the best years of a career lost to wartime military service and the difficulties of regaining a career undermined by the pettiness of the press, the prejudice within the game itself, the cowardice of baseball management, including the commissioner, and the financial and emotional struggle of surviving one more off-season and one more poor contract just to keep alive the fading dream of playing baseball one day in a major-league uniform.

Asinof's *Man on Spikes,* while detailed and comprehensive as a narrative, is not, however, a completely realistic portrait of Mike Kutner's life and career. When Kutner finally gets his chance to play in the major leagues, the narrative unfortunately turns to conventional bases-loaded, two-out, bottom-of-the-ninth, pennant-race dramatics for its conclusion. Even though Kutner fails in the clutch by striking out, the contrived climax of the novel's final chapter sounds a false note that plays itself out in Kutner's melodramatic rage at his failure, the comforting moral sentiments of the old-time baseball scout, and the final emotional reconciliation between Kutner and his wife: "You ain't a failure, no matter what they say. I can tell you that. You ain't a failure."

Asinof's own failure to sustain his realistic narrative in the final chapter of *Man on Spikes* is an unfortunate flaw, but it does not greatly diminish the achievement of the novel, its accurately detailed and comprehensive vision of the life and career of a baseball player. If anything, the heightened dramatics of Kutner's first and only major-league game and the stilted moralizing and emotions of the novel's last scenes are a reminder of the difficulty of writing a realistic novel within the romantic tradition of baseball fiction. In *Man on Spikes,* Asinof's narrative, through thirteen different points of view, resists the powerful emotional pull of baseball's dreaminess. Only when the novel finally shifts to the ballplayer's own perspective does the narrative take on the trappings of moral romance, and, when it does, it cloaks Mike Kutner's fate in the same emotional and moral glow, the same aura of innocence and goodness that surrounds Joe Jackson at the conclusion of Asinof's *Eight Men Out.*

In Eric Rolfe Greenberg's *The Celebrant,* the realistic baseball novel finally appears to achieve a perfect balance between subject and form, though the ending of *The Celebrant* also presents some problems. Rolfe's novel, unlike Asinof's *Man on Spikes,* responds to the challenge of the romantic tradition of baseball fiction by making that tradition the focus of its narrative. In place of the obscure and struggling Mike Kutner and his hard-bitten baseball career, Rolfe selects as his subject the legendary Christy Mathewson, baseball's seemingly purest hero, and his brilliant if star-crossed career. Instead of a narrative made up of shifting and often ironic perspectives, *The Celebrant,* living up to its title, glorifies, through the eyes of its hero-worshipping narrator, Mathewson's career from the occasion of his first no-hitter in 1901 to his death in 1925. Greenberg's narrative, however, rather than falling victim to hero-worshipping, balances, through most of the novel, the adoration of gifted ballplayers as gods with an understanding and appreciation of the aesthetic value of the game. The rarest of narrators in baseball fiction, Jack Kapp, the original designer of championship baseball rings, has the imaginative sensibility to recognize greatness of form on the playing field and the moral intelligence to understand the value of integrity in baseball's performers. He also has the comprehensive vision to appreciate both baseball's multiple perspectives and its simple design and purpose:

> To be a pitcher! I thought. A pitcher, standing at the axis of event, or a catcher with the God-view of play all before him; to be a shortstop, lord of the infield, or a center fielder with unchallenged claim to all the territory one's speed and skill could command; to perform the spontaneous acrobatics of the third baseman or the practiced ballet of the man at second, or to run and throw with the absolute commitment of the outfielder! And to live in a world without grays, where all decisions were final: ball or strike, safe or out, the game won or lost beyond question or appeal.

Rolfe's own artistry in *The Celebrant* is evident in the novel's sustained narrative of the relationship between Kapp and Mathewson from its initial stage of pure hero-worship, through its aesthetic period of mutual appreciation, to its final moment of moral revelation and spiritual epiphany. As the relationship moves through each phase, Rolfe strengthens his narrative by grounding the story of baseball's purest hero and its most adoring fan in the key historical moments of Mathewson's career from his no-hit performance against St. Louis on July 15, 1901, to his witnessing of the Black Sox scandal in 1919. He also adds depth to his narrative by placing his celebratory relationship within the larger historical context of the Progressive era and the booming rise of baseball and business in America at the beginning of the century.

The historical dimensions of *The Celebrant* add moral depth and emotional complexity to the narrative and to Rolfe's vision of the aesthetically balanced relationship between the inspired Kapp and the inspiring Mathewson. While Kapp, Rolfe's artist of the beautiful, sees Mathewson as the pure embodiment of his youthful dream of becoming a major-league pitcher and celebrates Mathewson's brilliant performances with marvelously designed and crafted rings, he is also aware of the vulgar integration of baseball with big business and the dangerous relationship between baseball and gambling. While Mathewson, Rolfe's artist of the game, embodies everything that is civilized and noble about baseball, he also recognizes the primitive brutality lurking beneath the simplicity, grace, and clarity of the game. The narrative even provides alter egos for Kapp in his brothers Eli and Arthur and for Mathewson in his manager John McGraw. Kapp's artistry and integrity are constantly threatened by Eli's lust for gambling and Arthur's appetite for making money. McGraw's combative drive and coarse behavior not only counter the heroic nobility of Mathewson, they draw out Mathewson's own warrior instinct on the field of play and actually seem much more in keeping with the brawling nature of the time.

Within this added complexity, the narrative of *The Celebrant* develops two stories that merge at dramatic moments in Mathewson's career and finally fuse at the most critical juncture in baseball history. The main narrative thread follows the story of Jack Kapp's struggle against the gambling and greed of his brothers and his determination to preserve the ideals he embraced as a young boy after hearing a speech, ghost-written by Mathewson, "analogizing baseball and life. Practice, dedication, clean living and fair play—these guaranteed success on and off the field." *The Celebrant,* however, also follows the story of Mathewson's career from the romantic heights of a no-hitter and a championship season, through the dramatic turmoil of the Merkle boner and the Snodgrass misplay, to the terrible tragedy of his final years, climaxed by Mathewson's discovery of the 1919 World Series fix. What emerges for the reader out of the two narrative strands is an understanding and appreciation, best expressed in the novel by Hugh Fullerton, of the baseball celebrant and the baseball hero: "The world makes you a god and hates you for being human, and if you plea for understanding it hates you all the more. Heroes are never forgiven their success, still less their failure. . . . All the celebrants of his work. We make the greatest demands. Every time he pitches I find myself hoping for the most extraordinary achievement, for my immortality lies in his."

Fullerton's insight into the relationship of the celebrant and the hero is dramatized in the novel's controversial final scene between Kapp, earlier described by Fullerton as "the high priest . . . the celebrant-in-chief," and the now dying Mathewson. In a scene that runs dangerously close to surrendering the narrative to the most extreme form of hero-worship, Kapp, after risking his own soul to save his brother from gamblers, is himself saved by Mathewson, who, in his final narrative moment, damns the Black Sox players and exhorts his celebrant not to abandon baseball's greatest player in his hour of agony: "'Look at me. Look into my eyes. Think of this: they diced for His robe while He suffered on the cross. Will you do that while I lay dying? No, you will not. No matter what may follow, you will not do that. Not you,' he whispered. 'Not you.'"

Among the fictions of baseball, among the fantastical narratives of extraordinary characters, incredible plots, and improbable endings, among the moral romances and tragedies with their baseball heroes, conventional dramatics, and life lessons, *The Celebrant* stands out for its singular expression of the artistry of the game, the brilliance and true greatness of its legends, and the devotion and integrity of its celebrants. And of all the baseball immortals, green heroes, and aging veterans celebrated in baseball novels, Greenberg's Christy Mathewson stands out on fiction's playing fields as the one true Player, whose pitching perfection, purity of character, and quiet dignity in the face of physical, emotional, and spiritual suffering are testament to the celebrant's belief that baseball, for the true believer, embodies no less than the romantic dream of lost youth and often is the source of comfort and inspiration for overcoming personal and national tragedies.

Yet *The Celebrant,* with all its nobility, grace, and vision, is, like *Man on Spikes* with its balance, comprehensiveness, and insight, an exception among conventional baseball novels, where the game of baseball is often a reflection of the game of life, where the baseball dream routinely transforms players into heroes and legends, and where baseball's readers can indulge their romantic fantasies while picking up lessons on the value of moral conduct and the virtue of having a good heart. For all the claims of Mark Harris for a tradition of realism and for all the accomplishments of Asinof and Greenberg in writing serious novels, baseball's own romantic tradition with its dream narrative still reigns over the baseball fictional landscape and still invites fairy-tale narratives, moral romances, and romantic tragedies.

TOZER, LOS ANGELES, P. C. L.

◆ 8 ◆

Jackie Robinson and the
Serious Baseball Novel

Though not included in Mark Harris's catalog of subjects for the serious baseball novel, America's racial intolerance and discrimination became a topic once baseball fiction began its realistic tradition. Reduced to harsh racial stereotypes and excluded from America's literary playing fields by dime novels and series books, African Americans finally became integrated within the pages of baseball novels once Jackie Robinson crossed Major League Baseball's color line in 1947 and baseball writers brought a more realistic perspective to writing fiction. While still excluded from symbolic and mythic baseball novels like Malamud's *The Natural,* African-American ballplayers finally began to cross the color line in baseball's fictional landscape with the publication of *The Southpaw* and the beginning of what Harris claims to be the realistic tradition of the baseball novel.

The influence of Jackie Robinson on the writing of *The Southpaw* becomes evident as soon as Henry Wiggen leaves home and heads south to his first professional training camp. When he arrives late at night and asks the security guard if anyone else is in camp yet, the guard tells him: "No . . . There is one n——r. He is in the same barrackses as you." Wiggen's meeting with Perry Simpson, also in his first professional season with the New York Mammoths, sets the stage in *The Southpaw* for Wiggen to learn something about racial discrimination as part of his education into manhood. As Wiggen and Simpson develop a close friendship at training camp, are assigned to the same minor-league team, and become roommates the following year, at least for a while, in their first big-league season, Wiggen as narrator observes the discrimination directed at Simpson and, on a few occasions, finds that discrimination directly aimed at him.

At training camp, Wiggen notes that once workouts started Simpson "did not go out and eat on account of the regulations," which Wiggen regards as "pretty damn scurvy." When the Mammoths play in Washington, a city Wiggen hates, he loses a roommate because "Perry must go sleep in Howard University." Wiggen also notes that it "would have been the same in St. Louis," if the Mammoth manager hadn't known the owner of the hotel where the team was staying. While Wiggen is willing to room with the "first colored Mammoth" since 1947 and doesn't mind posing with his arm around Simpson for a photographer from a Harlem newspaper, he runs into some heckling on the field because he "rooms with the n——r." Wiggen, however, who apparently possesses a kind of innate or innocent tolerance, either ignores the taunts or, when they become too vicious, gives the opposing bench "the old sign, a finger up."

Perry Simpson is clearly modeled after Jackie Robinson, though, unlike Robinson, he becomes a bench player, used mostly as a pinch runner, in his first season with the Mammoths. Like Robinson, Simpson was born in Georgia but moved to the Far West for a better life. He plays a solid defensive game at second base, but his real strength is the way he rattles the other team's pitcher when he gets on base: "You can't judge Perry by averages. The way you judge him is by the

number of times he gets on base, whether bunting or drawing a walk
or beating out a roller that on most fellows would be an out, and you
got to judge him by the way he keeps the opposition worried."

As for Simpson's friendship with Henry Wiggen, it's actually modeled more after the literary relationship between the runaway slave Jim
and Huck Finn than any real-life relationship. While Simpson experiences some of the same racial hatred and discrimination encountered
by Robinson in his first major-league season, his primary role in *The
Southpaw* is to serve as a sidekick and moral conscience to Wiggen.
The incidents of racial bigotry in *The Southpaw* are real enough, but
they serve only as part of the moral education of Wiggen, who grows
into manhood by novel's end. Simpson's role is so secondary and ex-
pendable that when the narrative reaches the climactic last month of
the pennant race, Mark Harris brings up another African American
from the minors to replace Wiggen as Simpson's roommate: "Perry and
Keith went their own way, and off the field I almost never seen them."
With Perry Simpson now segregated from the narrative, the last chapters, without the distraction of racial intolerance and injustice, play
out the Mammoths' championship season as Wiggen overcomes his
moral mistakes and his errors of judgment, learns something about
human nature and himself, and wins his manhood as well as Most
Valuable Player and Player of the Year honors.

When Mark Harris disposes of Perry Simpson as Henry Wiggen's
roommate, the plot contrivance echoes beyond *The Southpaw* because
Simpson is replaced by Bruce Pearson, the athlete dying young in
Harris's next novel. In *Bang the Drum Slowly*, often praised as one of
baseball's best novels, Harris continues the education of Henry Wiggen
but, without the social realism provided by a character like Perry Simpson, the novel never really strays far from the genre of the moral romance. Emotionally sentimental and morally instructive, *The Southpaw* fails to sustain and *Bang the Drum Slowly* avoids altogether the
social realism that would have made the novels more convincing as
fiction. Harris's sequel to *The Southpaw* would have been far differ-

ent and perhaps far more realistic if it had returned to the relationship between Henry Wiggen and Perry Simpson and focused its theme of responsibility and loyalty on race relations within the context of America's National Game.

The problem in *The Southpaw* is that the personal relationship between Henry Wiggen and Perry Simpson and Simpson's presence in the Mammoth clubhouse are never a part of the conflicts or challenges Wiggen faces on his way to manhood. The moral education of Henry Wiggen simply does not include facing his own ignorance of race relations or defending Simpson against the racial bigotry of their teammates. Perry Simpson, listed as wearing number 42 in a special opening-day scorecard, makes an appearance in *Bang the Drum Slowly,* but in his only significant scene the hard feelings between Simpson and Wiggen over Bruce Pearson, a white southerner, lead to a complete severing of their relationship.

In Eliot Asinof's *Man on Spikes,* published two years after *The Southpaw,* the issue of race does become a crucial part of a remarkably balanced and intimate study of the various forces at play in the life and career of a professional ballplayer. For Mike Kutner, the racial integration of baseball and its inherent prejudices and hypocrisy becomes yet another obstacle in his sixteen-year quest to play in the major leagues. In a chapter titled "The Negro," Kutner is forced to move from center field to left field for his Triple A Minneapolis team because the parent Chicago club wants to advance Ben Franks—"Move the big nigger in there and see what he can do"—so it can cash in on Brooklyn's success: "Up in Chicago, Jim Mellon had his eyes on Brooklyn, shifting from the gate receipts to Robinson's ability and back to the gate receipts. The black man was being accepted and the ball club was making a fat dollar for its 'crusade.' So Jim Mellon had to get himself a black man."

Asinof's chapter is particularly striking and insightful because its narrative reflects Ben Franks's perspective rather than Mike Kutner's. From Franks's perspective, the reader of *Man on Spikes* encounters far more than Kutner's reaction to Franks's presence on the team. Asinof's narrative records the "hoarse, rasping voice of hate" heard from the stands and the opposing bench and the deeply felt and expressed resentment of Franks's teammates. It also captures Franks's own feelings as he endures viciousness on the field and ostracism in the clubhouse. As Franks tries to cope with the "monster of hate and pressure," he thinks about "Jackie Robinson up there breaking in with Brooklyn" and realizes that a black man "would have to be pretty terrific to stick, not just good enough." He also realizes that his own owner, up in Chicago, believes that "Robinson seemed the wrong kind of black boy to bring up. Too smart, too aggressive, too tricky. His feet were too small. The public might not like too much of that. But a big, lumbering quiet boy who can blast that long ball. The crowds would really go for that."

Knowing he is hated and exploited, Franks struggles to be good enough on the field and, when given the brief opportunity off the field, is capable of expressing his gratitude for the Negro League players who, while denied the opportunity, prepared the way to the major leagues for others. He remembers Josh Gibson—"ten times the ballplayer Ben was"—and how badly Gibson wanted to play in the majors. He also tells Kutner and one of his teammates about the wonderful skills and accomplishments of Satchel Paige, who "left a trail of goose eggs across a good slice of the country" despite the difficult playing conditions in the Negro Leagues and the remarkable talent of some of the players.

What Franks finally realizes, however, is that Kutner and his teammates, rather than hating him because of his race, resent him because they are afraid of the black players "coming up, wondering if there was a mess of them who might beat [them] out." Franks even reaches an understanding and acceptance of sorts with Kutner. When confronted by Franks for showing him up in the outfield, Kutner first tells Franks that he was due to go up to the majors next spring until he was forced to move from center field to left field to make room for Franks. When

Franks bitterly complains that he is not being treated fairly as a ball-player because of the color of his skin, Kutner takes off his glasses and tells Franks: "See these stinking things . . . I got troubles of my own."

Franks's understanding that Kutner has struggled throughout his career against another kind of prejudice changes nothing in the rivalry between the two, but when they collide in the outfield, Kutner defends Franks by telling their teammates the collision was his fault. This crucial act of responsibility on the field drains the hatred, at least for the moment, from the faces of the other players and draws Franks and Kutner together as they walk off the field. When Franks hands Kutner his bent but unbroken glasses, the two appear to recognize each other's determination to overcome the prejudices that would deny or exploit their dreams of playing in the major leagues.

While Asinof never wrote a sequel to *Man on Spikes,* he did write a later novel with an African-American ballplayer as its central character. Unfortunately, *The Bedfellow,* published twelve years after *Man on Spikes,* has little to offer about baseball. When the novel begins, Mike Sorrell has quit the game in his prime rather than accept a trade that would have sent him from New York to Atlanta and undermined his planned interracial marriage. With Sorrell retired, the only opportunities in *The Bedfellow* for insights into the racial tensions in baseball and the status of black ballplayers in the 1960s come about through Sorrell's recollections. At an early point in the novel, for example, Sorrell recalls how African Americans "were an integral part of every club, traveled together, dressed in the same locker room, played together, showered together. But off the field, we remained separate. An integrated-segregated split-screen colorvision show. We ate separately, roomed separately, socialized separately. And though it was not a necessity, essentially, that was the way it was. Baseball had broken the color line, but it couldn't abide Brotherhood."

The problem in *The Bedfellow* is that the reader never experiences baseball's "integrated-segregated split-screen colorvision show." Instead the narrative follows Sorrell through a series of miscalculations and misadventures as he travels through the sophisticated white man's world of Madison Avenue and upper-crust New York society. The only time Sorrell plays ball is at a pick-up softball game in Central Park that turns into a mockery of Sorrell's baseball talent and career when he is given a second chance after making an out to hit the game-winning home run and act out the adolescent fantasy for the "Sunday morning athletes," for their "amusement of seeing the anticipated actually happen, I suppose, a big free bubbly show with celebrities and folklore and happy ending, all wrapped up into one lusty climax."

Other than visits to ex-teammates, one a bigoted white, the other his black former roommate, Sorrell's journey focuses on his rebellion against the corruption and deception of the liberal white world and on his eventual acceptance, signified by his decision not to return to playing baseball, of hypocrisy and duplicity as the inherent conditions of integration: "So, the great conspiracy is all rounded out. Its power seems almost without limit, complete with all races and creeds, all moralities, legal and otherwise, and, that, I suppose, is the essence of integration." Its power is also too much for Mike Sorrell, who surrenders his dreams and his pride for a return to the good life: "Then I weaved over all the debris, thankful for the destruction of that mirror, for the last thing I want to do is look at myself."

The missed opportunities of Mark Harris and Eliot Asinof to write novels that do more than use the African-American ballplayer to embellish the moral education of a white ballplayer or to use baseball merely as a narrative contrivance to draw attention to the societal and political conditions of black/white relationships in America are typical of the serious or adult baseball novel. In Martin Quigley's *Today's Game* (1965), a novel that focuses on one day and one crucial midseason game in the life of a baseball manager, Barney Mann has placed his job and career in jeopardy by trading Jerry Adams, his best friend and "most effective righthanded pitcher in baseball . . . for a young Negro outfielder who still had his ability and himself to prove." Rather than drawing out the racial implications of the resistance of the "Old

Liners" to the trade and the pressures on the newly acquired Bill Wellington, the narrative emphasizes the unorthodox strategies used by Mann to defeat his old friend. While Mann knows and regrets "that baseball is a game in which personal and even racial and religious hatreds were factors" and recognizes the dissension race has caused in his own clubhouse, his attention is on winning today's game and using the skills of his players—Wellington ends the game with a wall-crashing catch—to achieve that end.

In John Hough Jr.'s *The Conduct of the Game* (1986), the African-American ballplayer is more angry, aggressive, and outspoken, but his role in the narrative is secondary, only a part of the moral education of first-year major-league umpire Lee Malcolm. Appearing at the mid-point of the novel, Ron Chapman, also in his first season in the major leagues, is a Jackie Robinson for the sixties. Educated at UCLA, arrested in Montgomery, Alabama, "for sitting in the whites-only section of a city bus," and a personal friend of Martin Luther King Jr., Chapman forces Malcolm to recognize the racism that exists in baseball and influences decision making on and off the field. This recognition, like Malcolm's coming to terms with the homosexuality of one of his fellow umpires, is played out in the conventional coming-of-age narrative of baseball as a moral and emotional testing ground.

In Barry Beckham's *Runner Mack* (1972), often designated as the only serious or adult baseball novel written by an African American, the political awakening and education of Henry Adams, an African-American ballplayer who dreams of playing in the major leagues, is the essence of the narrative. The African-American experience is central to the narrative, as Henry Adams learns from the black militant Runner Mack that he will never realize his dream as long as American society is controlled by whites. The problem in *Runner Mack*, however, is that, like Asinof's *The Bedfellow,* baseball becomes secondary, more a source for metaphors in a narrative much more concerned with raising social and political consciousness than with racial issues inside baseball itself. The only time Henry Adams plays baseball is at a tryout with "the Stars, the American baseball team." In a surrealistic episode, Adams is forced to hit against a pitching machine turned up to 150 miles-per-hour and field against another machine that fires howitzer shots into the outfield. Even though Adams manages to hit and field impressively, the episode is unreal. The baseball field merely becomes a symbol for an American society that turns dreams into nightmares for African Americans. Heavily symbolic and surrealistic, *Runner Mack* is more an attempt to rewrite Ellison's *Invisible Man* for the postmodern era than a realistic portrait of the African-American ballplayer.

Ironically, several baseball novels written in the postmodern era about African Americans, rather than offering a portrait of black players in the post-Robinson world of baseball, have gone back to the Negro barnstorming teams in the pre-Robinson era. With the exception of William Brashler's *The Bingo Long Traveling All-Stars and Motor Kings* (1973), the novels use the experiences of Negro barnstorming teams to teach a white character something about racial intolerance and bigotry. In Martin Quigley's *The Original Colored House of David* (1981), the narrative follows a white youth, frustrated by his family's and the town's unwillingness to treat him as a grown-up, as he goes on the road to prove himself. As Speedy, the deaf-dumb albino, he faces the same prejudices as his teammates, though in Quigley's coming-of-age novel there are no real violent confrontations. Speedy's real lesson is that, while he may play for the Original Colored House of David, he knows little about the life of African Americans in America and even less about the history of Negro baseball.

In another moral romance about a Negro barnstorming team, John Craig's *Chappie and Me* (1979), a white young adult catches on with Chappie Johnson and His Colored All-Stars when the team comes up short of players. While there is one serious racial confrontation in the novel and a bit of unnecessary melodrama when a tornado injures a few of the players, the narrative, told by Joe Gillen, who first wears black shoe polish, then lampblack, when he plays first base, is a bittersweet, often nostalgic retrospective of the All-Stars' "family feeling and the closeness and what we shared." The novel ends only when the All-Stars head south and the narrator, a Canadian, decides that, with the outbreak of the Second World War, "it was time to go home."

In Jay Neugeboren's *Sam's Legacy* (1973) and Jerome Charyn's *The Seventh Babe* (1979), the narratives are symbolic and ambitious, but the role of Negro barnstorming remains essentially the same. In *Sam's Legacy*, the interior narrative, titled "My Life and Death in the Negro American Baseball League: A Slave Narrative," is a radical, revisionist memoir of Mason Tidewater's turbulent years as the "Black Babe" of Negro baseball, his obsession and eventual love affair with Babe Ruth, and his subsequent flight from baseball after he strangles a teammate to death because he deliberately cost Tidewater a perfect no-hitter against an all-star team of white major leaguers. Tidewater's memoir, written in a basement room used in the past to hide runaway slaves, is itself encased within the larger narrative of Sam Berman's struggle against his unlucky streak as a gambler and his legacy of stories and memories from his Jewish father and grandfather. While Tidewater's story is the most compelling part of *Sam's Legacy*, Tidewater's role in the novel is to offer himself up as a surrogate father and to give Sam Berman an alternative legacy, one that Sam ultimately rejects because he believes Tidewater, unlike Sam's own father, has made a testament out of his loss of faith and his flight from himself, his people, and the world of baseball. At novel's end, Sam Berman imagines that soon after Mason Tidewater vanishes, "a group of elderly black men" will appear to say "they had been looking for a man whom they believed had once been their teammate."

In *The Seventh Babe*, Negro barnstorming once again plays a significant role in the narrative, but only as a subterranean world for Babe Ragland, cursed for being the seventh Babe to play for the Boston Red Sox after Babe Ruth and eventually banned by Judge Landis for unwittingly consorting with a gambler. Once Ragland joins the Cincinnati Colored Giants, however, he leaves history behind and enters a talismanic and timeless world where, accompanied by a hunchback dwarf, he encounters magical events and legendary players. A left-handed third baseman of unlimited range, Ragland eventually becomes primordial in appearance and wizard-like in skills, the stuff of myth himself. As Negro barnstorming begins "to suffocate," Ragland and his team, now "baseball dinosaurs," continue to play baseball, which has now become more imagined than real in the narrative, an incurable "disease in the magician's head."

Unlike *The Seventh Babe*, Brashler's *The Bingo Long Traveling All-Stars and Motor Kings* is grounded in the real history of Negro barnstorming. The novel's main characters, Bingo Long and Leon Carter, are modeled after Negro League greats Josh Gibson and Satchel Paige. Its detailed description of the All-Stars' clowning and their ability to survive unbearable road conditions and intolerant racial attitudes also gives an air of credibility to the narrative. Even the break-up of the outlaw All-Stars is grounded in baseball history, as the team's best young players are signed to minor-league contracts in anticipation of the integration of Organized Baseball. Yet Brashler's novel, for all its historical underpinnings, remains a picaresque tale of roguish heroes and vagabond adventures. There is no white narrator or central figure to reduce the novel to a moral romance, but the narrative celebrates the camaraderie of the All-Stars and closes on a clearly sentimental and nostalgic note, as Bingo Long wistfully regrets that he "was born too quick" to play in the major leagues.

This narrative tendency to incorporate and subsume the experiences of African-American ballplayers into revisionist histories or moral romances has continued in baseball fiction with the publication of Mark Winegardner's *The Veracruz Blues* (1996) and Peter Hamill's *Snow in August* (1997). In *The Veracruz Blues*, the story of Theolic "Fireball" Smith, a proud and bitter Negro League star pitcher who dreamed of being the first African American to cross baseball's color line, provides an important inside narrative and serves as a reminder of the exclusion of black ballplayers from baseball history and its traditional narratives.

But the novel's main purpose is to transform the Mexican League's raid on the American major leagues into a precursor to the unionization of baseball and the elimination of the reserve clause.

In *Snow in August,* Jackie Robinson's crossing of baseball's color line merely embellishes the coming-of-age narrative of the friendship between Michael Devlin, an Irish Catholic youth, and Rabbi Hirsch, a friendship that overcomes cultural and religious barriers as well as an anti-Semitic gang of local toughs. While the novel clearly displays Robinson as a guiding light for tolerance and understanding, the fight that breaks out between racist fans and union workers at Ebbets Field and the physical force conjured up to dispatch the anti-Semitic toughs suggest that something more than goodness of heart and spiritual enlightenment are needed in a world in which racial, ethnic, and religious understanding is as rare as snow in August.

Hamill's *Snow in August* is reminiscent of an earlier coming-of-age novel, Robert Mayer's *The Grace of Shortstops* (1984), which, set in 1947, also exploits Jackie Robinson as an inspiration for racial and ethnic tolerance and understanding. Its young hero, Peewee Brunig, takes heart from Robinson's integration of baseball because he wants to be the first Jewish shortstop in the majors. Robinson's presence in the novel, however, fades early as Peewee, whose role model obviously is Peewee Reese, survives several family crises by acting with the grace of shortstops and the courage of catchers, but not with the character of second basemen.

Fifty years after Jackie Robinson crossed Organized Baseball's color line, his historical act still influences the baseball novel, but the results of that influence remain as unsatisfactory as Robinson's impact on baseball itself. While numerous African Americans have now appeared on the playing fields of baseball and baseball fiction, their experiences have often been perceived as important not in themselves but as moral or historical lessons for whites. Part of the problem in baseball fiction, of course, is the almost total absence of baseball novels written by African Americans, but equally problematic is the expropriation and exploitation of African-American ballplayers, from Negro League barnstormers to Jackie Robinson, to serve baseball's self-congratulatory perception of itself as representing the best qualities of American society, its democratic spirit, its fundamental goodness and rightness of character, and its innate sense of fair play. This perception of baseball as synonymous with the American Dream seems, however, oddly out of focus for those excluded or segregated from the baseball dream for so long and who still wait for a more realistic lens to give the proper perspective and rightful place to their experiences in the history of baseball.

◆ 9 ◆

Barbarians at the Plate: The Postmodern Baseball Writer

CASTLETON, LOS ANGELES, P. C. L.

Important baseball books written between the Vietnam era and our current generation have played a major role, because of their success with readers, in shifting attention away from the enjoyment and appreciation of baseball to the problems inside the game and the shortcomings of its players and owners. These postmodern baseball narratives, unlike their more traditional counterparts, have anticipated, helped define, and continue to explore and perhaps even exploit the disillusionment and cynicism surrounding baseball today.

While W. P. Kinsella and Donald Hall have perpetuated the mythology of baseball with magical stories and personal essays about fathers playing catch with sons, postmodern novels, ranging from Vietnam-era metafiction like Coover's *Universal Baseball Association* and Roth's *Great American Novel* to David James Duncan's antiwar *The Brothers K,* have offered readers a darker vision of baseball grounded in self-absorption, self-betrayal, and self-destruction. For every lyrical or moral expression by Roger Angell, Thomas Boswell, Roger Kahn, or George Will celebrating the value, meaning, or craft of baseball, there have been postmodern narratives, ranging from Bouton's irreverent *Ball Four* to revisionist works such as John Helyar's *Lords of the Realm* and Al Stump's *Cobb,* that have questioned baseball's values, debunked the game's legends, and exposed the moral mistakes responsible for baseball's current plight.

Stephen Jay Gould claims that the catalyst for the development of the postmodern in biographical writing was Jim Bouton's *Ball Four:* "The change to kiss-and-tell biography would have occurred in any case. . . . But particular items fuel or catalyze any particular transition, and we need to honor these efforts whatever the general inevitability." While the evolution of the kiss-and-tell biography would eventually reduce *Ball Four* from shocking revelation to entertaining but dated artifact, Bouton's book has the key element of the postmodern baseball narrative. The central figure of baseball's postmodern world is typically the outsider, the rebel, or, in Bouton's case, the baseball "deviant." In *Ball Four* the deviant is the ballplayer who breaks the most traditional rule of major-league baseball: "What you say here, what you do here, let it stay here, when you leave here."

Bouton's deviant serves up no season-in-the-sun narrative extolling the heroic performance of a star player or the epic achievement of a championship ball club. Rather than celebrating the heroic, Bouton's narrative rejects baseball's "indiscriminate hero-making." Instead of placing ballplayers within the epic, *Ball Four* tells the tale of "pettiness in baseball, and meanness and stupidity beyond belief," of back-stabbing and pill-popping ballplayers, incompetent and mean-spirited coaches, managers, and general managers, vindictive umpires, and Baseball Annies. While holding on to his boyhood love of the game, Bouton narrates his struggle to play another season in the major leagues, this time with an expansion team. Still dreaming the conventional baseball dream of winning the final game of his team's championship season, Bouton records the boredom and mindlessness of the long season, the pettiness and hypocrisy routinely displayed in the clubhouse, and the alienation and retribution suffered by those who do not conform to baseball's orthodoxy: "One of the things that none of us should do, [the commissioner] said, is knock the game. . . . In other words, don't say anything bad about baseball."

What gives added definition to Bouton's portrait of the baseball player as deviant, beyond the act of defying baseball's totems and taboos and telling the truth about the conduct of the game, is the narrative's awareness of temporal events outside of baseball. Unlike books mythologizing baseball as timeless, *Ball Four* plays out Bouton's season of struggle and discontent within the political and social unrest of 1969. In doing so, it places baseball politics and Bouton's deviant ballplayer within the broader perspective and context of the country's civil rights struggle and the student protests against the Vietnam War. Trying to overcome his reputation as an outsider and a troublemaker, Bouton identifies himself with the black ballplayer who, more than twenty years after Jackie Robinson crossed baseball's color line, still has to overcome racial prejudice and racial quotas, "still has to be better than his white counterparts to do as well." At odds with baseball's establishment, short-haired and uniformed Bouton finds common cause with students concerned about more than baseball: "So they wear long hair and sandals and have dirty feet. I can understand why. It's a badge, a sign they are different from people who don't care. . . . So I wanted to tell everyone, 'Look, I'm with you baby. I understand. Underneath my haircut I really understand that you're doing the right thing.'"

Important postmodern biographies of two of baseball's greatest stars have also grounded their legendary subjects in history, but in entirely different ways. In *Babe: The Legend Comes to Life*, Robert W. Creamer has to historicize a ballplayer who is more legend than life. Recognizing that, like all legends, "Ruth's had a strong vein of truth in it—and an equally strong vein of baloney," Creamer sees his task as producing "a total biography, one that, hopefully, would present all the facts and myths." Creamer achieves his goal and writes a masterful biography by undermining the glorification of Ruth and getting at the truth behind the myths—sometimes a myth turns out to be true—

and by allowing the greatness of Ruth's career and the gargantuan nature of his life to speak for themselves. The result is a biography not for boys, though it details the childlike qualities of Ruth's character, and not a sensational exposé, though it never avoids Ruth's "many and glaring" sins. At one point, Creamer writes that when he had to, Ruth "could discipline himself, and he had a continuing sense of responsibility to certain people and certain things, among them his own position as Hero." Creamer's biography, in its own way, is a disciplined and responsible narrative that never debunks baseball's greatest hero but, down to its remarkable flat-line ending, never betrays itself by choosing the myth over the life.

In *Willie's Time,* Charles Einstein faces a different problem—capturing the life and career of a ballplayer who was perhaps the greatest athlete in the history of baseball but seemed incapable of carrying his on-the-field heroics over into the turbulent social and political challenges of his time. Einstein's narrative of Willie Mays, which received a Pulitzer Prize nomination for biography, more accurately describes itself as "a memoir" in its historizing of Mays's life and times. Its narrative skillfully weaves the elements of Einstein's own career as a reporter covering Mays and the critical social and political events of the years covering five American presidents from Truman to Nixon into the most dramatic moments of Mays's career. The result is a lively and compelling portrait of Mays's greatness as a ballplayer within the larger context of the country's radical social and political changes, especially in the area of civil rights. There is a danger in personalizing baseball history and biography—as Seymour proved in his baseball histories—because the writer can slip too easily into the role of a fan or an apologist, but Einstein, with only a few lapses, manages to bring Willie's time to life without avoiding the social controversies of Mays's life or extending the glorification of Mays's real heroics within the game: "Is it true that sooner or later the gods of mythology become their own best customers?"

Doing the right thing in the postmodern baseball narrative often means deviating from the traditional view of baseball as America's game and its players as larger than life in their greatness. This deviation from tradition is especially striking in postmodern baseball histories and biographies because it reflects such a radical shift from the standard or conventional tendency of these narratives toward storytelling and hagiography. Helyar's postmodernist *Lords of the Realm,* rather than narrating baseball as fable or epic, offers what he describes as "the real history of baseball" and a counterstatement to the historizing of baseball as America's national game and its players as the embodiment of the American Dream. In Helyar's revisionist historical approach, baseball's golden eras, its "age of innocence," are reduced to an opening chapter or a historical prelude noting the passage of baseball from a game to a national pastime and a big business ruled by baseball owners, "the masters of all they surveyed, the Lords of the Realm."

Helyar's history of baseball actually begins at the end of 1965 with the hiring of Marvin Miller as the director of the Players Association. For Helyar, in the beginning of real baseball history was the word, and the word was "union." *Lords of the Realm,* as a title, is really a misnomer because the book, with all its claims for reality, tells a carnivalesque story of the radicalization of the major-league baseball player and the demythologizing of the baseball owner and the commissioner. While Albert Spalding may have provided the ownership story of baseball history in *America's National Game,* Helyar offers a postmodern history in which owners, stripped of their traditional authority and their control of the game, are exposed as tyrants, scoundrels, and fools, and baseball, no longer wrapped in legends and dreams, is perceived as a commodity, governed by the talents of the players and the demands of the marketplace. Helyar's story of postmodern baseball suggests that baseball narratives, like all other narratives, are ideological, and once the owners' privileged and paternalistic history is noted and dismissed, a new player's ideology of revolution and fraternity emerges as baseball's one true historical narrative.

The only problem for Helyar is that his historical vision of a better baseball world, democratically inspired and market-driven, is undermined by the ideological assumptions and conditions of his own narrative. He would like to tell the story of the "amazing metamorphosis" of Marvin Miller "from functionary technician to dynamic leader, and the players, from compliant peons to budding rebels" and their overthrow of a baseball establishment run by tyrannical owners and their stooge commissioners—and he does, for the most part, in *Lords of the Realm*. Helyar's brave new baseball world, however, now rid of old owners' tales and driven by economic realities, becomes so destabilized by the greed that also threatened baseball's early history that it quickly descends into malice and chaos. Instead of a new democratic realm governed by the Great Emancipator and his revolutionaries, Helyar's narrative encounters a baseball Pandemonium: its revolutionaries now "horribly money conscious," its teams hopelessly divided by uneven television revenues into "haves and have nots," its new "caste system" ballparks built to accommodate rich and privileged fans, and the national pastime stricken by political anarchy and alienated from the American public.

The conclusion of Helyar's historical narrative resists its own overthrow and descent into chaos by gesturing toward the saving grace of the game's resiliency and appeal, the forgiveness of the fans, and "the glimmer of optimism" in negotiation and mediation; but, even with this misplaced optimism, Helyar's final vision remains Orwellian. If Helyar's *Lords of the Realm* is baseball's real history, then in baseball's new world ballplayers and owners share "many of their traits," despite Helyar's insistence that baseball's decline is still "the owner's own damn fault."

The narrative gap between Spalding's patriotic and moral tale of baseball's early history and Helyar's postmodern revisionist history has been filled by G. Edward White's *Creating the National Pastime*. Neither promotional nor subversive, White's historical narrative, focusing on baseball from 1903 to 1953, tells the story of baseball's modern transformation into the national pastime and why it may eventually and inevitably lose its unique and mythic status in American culture. Instead of dismissing Spalding's historical claim, White believes "that in one sense that claim is valid: baseball has been an especially meaningful sport for Americans because of its association with the past, and past time." Rather than resisting Helyar's Orwellian vision, White agrees that baseball's revolutionary change, while "dramatically improving the financial position of players, has thrown the game into chaos." He further suggests that this change may have jeopardized the game's elevated status as the national pastime by reducing baseball to the ordinary level of "entertainment business" and "sports industry," no different from "other contemporary sports."

A professor of history and law, White mediates his own historical narrative between the claims of Spalding and Helyar. While recognizing the illogical economics of baseball's frozen demographics and the unfairness and questionable legality of its labor practices, White also sees these "culturally and economically anachronistic features" as fundamental to baseball's unique position as the national pastime. White begins his narrative by tracing the origin of baseball's mythic status to the Progressive era in American history. As baseball came of age, with the growth and dynamics of American cities, its teams became the "focus of civic pride and energy," while the game itself "invoked rural and pastoral associations that were particularly evocative to a generation of Americans confronting an increasingly urbanizing and industrializing environment." For White, this historical paradox of baseball as a product of time and yet a metaphor for a lost past became its most defining characteristic for owners, players, writers, and fans and its most compelling force in shaping the game's cultural iconography.

In *Creating the National Pastime* White offers up a history in which baseball becomes both a major business enterprise and an essential cultural entity. In the Progressive era, baseball owners built steel and concrete ballparks that were intended to be "architectural landmarks in a growing urban landscape" and "permanent features of city life in twentieth-century America." To reinforce its growing status as a symbol of urban stability and civic pride, baseball also justified and exploited its notorious reserve clause to guarantee close competition and foster fan loyalty and support for the home team. When the Black Sox scandal threatened baseball's iconic role as a clean, wholesome, and respectable sport for the American public, baseball's magnates created the office of commissioner to protect the game's image as pure and uncorruptible. When threatened by the Great Depression, baseball responded by creating the All-Star Game and the Hall of Fame to draw attention to "the heroic dimensions of playing major league baseball and the continuity of the game over time."

As a cultural mirror of American society, baseball reflected the country's racial and ethnic discrimination, but it also served as a public arena for integration and assimilation. As the guardian of America's idyllic past, organized baseball resisted playing games at night as well as the broadcasting and televising of games; but once it gave in to these "unnatural" changes, it realized a broader audience and a dramatic growth in revenue. Yet, as baseball changed and became more of a media event, as it abandoned its territorial principle and moved struggling franchises to other cities, as it increased its profitability through lucrative media contracts and ironically created the atmosphere for a growing labor consciousness among players and for the eventual end of the reserve clause, it also began to lose its spirit of continuity with America's past and its special cultural status with the American people. With the loss of its anachronistic principles and practices, baseball also lost its claim to America's civic pride and its "memory of its rural, pastoral past." For White, baseball, once revered and celebrated for its timeless rituals and idyllic qualities, may now "increasingly be the stuff of history. It may be that the twenty-first century will be the one in which commentators gravely announce that baseball was, rather than is, the national pastime."

In an early chapter of *Creating the National Pastime,* White points out the major role played by earlier baseball commentators in fostering the public view of baseball as a noble game played by heroic figures, its narrative "a drama of epic proportions, with civic ramifications." He also notes that when some journalists, Ring Lardner, Paul Gallico, and Damon Runyon, for example, experienced a tension or conflict between their roles as reporters and celebrants, they abandoned journalism for fiction. White's suggestion that these writers turned to fiction to create a realistic counterpoint to the more common practice of mythologizing or romancing the game, however, is not supported by baseball fiction from the Progressive era to the beginning of the postmodern period. Not until the appearance of novels questioning the special status of baseball's myths, rituals, and legends did baseball fiction challenge and eventually destabilize the tradition and conventions of celebrating baseball as the national pastime and a cultural icon.

As impressive as Mark Harris's novels are, for example, in capturing the vernacular of baseball and the career struggles of its players, their narratives still rely upon typological and predictable baseball characters and situations and upon conventional strategies of fiction writing. As baseball entertainments, the novels take full advantage of the formulaic narrative of a baseball player of extraordinary talent playing out his personal conflict within the epic drama of tight pennant races and record-breaking performances. As literary events, the novels use baseball to narrate moral romances or fables about life's lessons.

It was with the appearance of Bernard Malamud's *The Natural* that fiction writers began to challenge rather than perpetuate the cultural icons and mythic narrations of baseball. At first glance, *The Natural* seems the perfect expression and confirmation of baseball's mythic status. Not only does it rely upon baseball's pantheon of heroes and legends, it places baseball's mythology within the universal context of vegetation myths and Greek legends. Yet Roy Hobbs, for all his knightly aspirations, undermines the mythmaking powers of baseball through his ignorance of tradition and his corruptibility. Rather than signifying the timeless and heroic in baseball, *The Natural* anticipates the postmodern text. As Deanne Westbrook points out in *Ground Rules,* her book on baseball and myth, "the mythic dimensions of Roy Hobbs's world are created by echo, allusion, suggestion, parody, and image, which are the hallmarks of a postmodern scene. The novel's mode is irony, its theme is terror, and Roy Hobbs is unmistakably a twentieth-century man."

One of the great narrative ironies of *The Natural* is the press's praise of Roy Hobbs: "He belonged, they wrote, with the other immortals, a giant in performance, who resembled the burly boys of the eighties and nineties more than the streamlined kids of today. He was a throwback to a time of true heroes . . . a natural." Roy Hobbs is a throwback, but not to a mythic age or an idyllic past. As a natural rather than mythic artifice he has great talent, but he also possesses or is possessed by the demonic vindictiveness of a Ty Cobb and the flagrant ignorance of a Joe Jackson. At novel's end Hobbs stands not on the threshold of the Hall of Fame but as a reminder of the megalomania and corruptibility that threatened the game even as it evolved into the national pastime and still threatens baseball in the postmodern world. To a youth's cry to "'Say it ain't true, Roy,'" Hobbs "wanted to say it wasn't but couldn't, and lifted his hands to his face and wept bitter tears," as the echo of the Black Sox scandal and not the echoing thunder of Wonderboy closes out Hobbs's career.

Malamud's *The Natural* anticipates postmodern baseball fiction in the way the narrative questions cultural and mythic assumptions about the nature of baseball. In later novels, writers go beyond challenging the seriousness of the conventions and tradition of baseball storytelling to mock the very process itself. In Coover's *Universal Baseball Association,* J. Henry Waugh invents a baseball dice league as compensation for his otherwise disgusting and dismal life, but when the invented history of Waugh's imaginary world is threatened by the fatal beaning of wunderkind Damon Rutherford, Waugh recovers from his despair only when he elevates the Universal Baseball Association to a religious allegory through the transformative power of a ritual beaning enacted each baseball season. The irony of Waugh's transformation of his dice league into a baseball religion, replete with its own sacred dramaturgy, is that the act in effect refines Waugh's own humanity out of existence and drains the joy out of baseball as a game.

In Philip Roth's *The Great American Novel,* the tendency of metafiction toward madness and mockery reaches the nethermost region of satirical rage and subversive parody. Roth adds the exaggerated dimension of social satire to his narrative, however, by seeing the fate of the Ruppert Mundys as a reflection of the prejudice, corruption, and exploitation inherent in baseball as a social enterprise, as well as a harbinger of the paranoia and greed of the postwar 1950s and the disruption and chaos of the early 1970s. While Roth's narrator, Word Smith, tells his wildly extravagant and darkly comic tale of a team and a league *"willfully erased from the national memory,"* Roth's narrative exposes the worst side of baseball imaginable at one of the most incompetent and depressing periods in its history. The Ruppert Mundys, as a baseball team, are Roth's collective Caliban, a team of alienated, raging, and deformed human beings, allowed to roam and perform on baseball fields, though denied a home park, because of the need to keep baseball going during the dark days of World War II. As baseball's team Caliban, the Mundys are also feared and hated as well as exploited and, once the war is over and they no longer serve the national purpose, the team is purposely erased from history, left behind and forgotten by everyone except the raging and vengeful Word Smith.

To rescue the Patriot League and its hero Luke Gofannon from historical oblivion, Word Smith decides to take "what America did to the Ruppert Mundys (and to me)" and make it into the Great American Novel. While Smith's attempt to restore a lost chapter to baseball history is noble enough, and his decision to write the Great American Novel about baseball is certainly ambitious enough, his own writing unfortunately is so exaggerated by rage and so distorted by paranoia that his effort to tell the truth about baseball is defeated not only by baseball's establishment but by the mad ramblings of Smith himself. Smith's madly alliterative style and its spirit of exaggeration work well in the journalistic service of baseball's own tendency toward legend, fable, and myth, but, when he turns his writing against baseball, his frenetic style and his ferocious doomsday prophecy serve only to alienate his writing and vision from the traditional narratives of baseball, especially its dream narrative. Just as Roy Hobbs falls victim to his own talent and J. Henry Waugh surrenders his humanity to his own invention, Word Smith exiles himself from baseball with his own writing style, a style so extravagant that it prevents him from being believed even when he thinks he is exposing the truth about baseball.

In David James Duncan's *The Brothers K,* the revisionist attempt to redefine America's historical perspective and redirect its vision of the future actually embraces baseball's mythic and transformative power. Spanning American history from the Korean War to the Vietnam War, the narrative of *The Brothers K* serves up the view of baseball as "inherently antiwar" and ballplayers as "basically just a bunch of unusually well-coordinated guys working hard and artfully to prevent wars, by making peace more interesting." In Duncan's postmodern vision of inclusion, baseball becomes less of a cultural icon and more of a cultural mode, capable of expressing our love of play, our "grateful hearts," our mindfulness of "the needs of others," and our "love for each other."

Duncan's antiwar narrative and his vision of baseball as America's peaceable kingdom is so inclusive that it even has room for Ty Cobb: "even warlike ballplayers fight for peace by making [baseball] more interesting." Duncan's view of Cobb, however, is far too radical for even the postmodern period of baseball narratives with its kiss-and-tell biographies, its revisionist and mediated histories, and its subversive fictions. In historical periods of cultural shiftings and radical changes, narratives often turn to the satanic or the apocalyptic to explain the disruption and chaos that appear to herald a new age. In the world of baseball this need to demonize has manifested itself in one of the game's greatest players. With Al Stump's *Cobb,* published nearly twenty-five years after Ty Cobb's *My Life in Baseball,* the postmodern baseball narrative has found its perfect monster. Stump's biography is a counternarrative to Cobb's own earlier text, in which he refutes his reputation as "a sadistic, slashing, swashbuckling despot, a Draco of the diamond" by portraying himself as an outcast hero revenging himself upon baseball's own villainy. Stump offers a postmodern biography of a Cobb who played like a demon because he was a demon. After observing Cobb's "acute self-worship, delusions of persecution, and more than a touch of dipsomania" and listening to Cobb's "confession of his most private thoughts, along with the details of his life," Stump authorizes himself to give the answer to the secret of Cobb's life: "Was Cobb psychotic throughout his baseball career? The answer is yes."

If, as some traditionalists suggest, baseball is rapidly descending into hell in a handbasket, it now apparently has Stump's Ty Cobb gleefully waiting with demonic gaze and flashing spikes for its arrival. This vision of baseball as paradise lost, however, still serves up the game as the stuff of epic narratives, or at least mock epics, just as Duncan's *Brothers K* holds up baseball as a cultural mirror, albeit a cracked one, of America's hope for a paradise regained after the tragedy of the Vietnam War. As baseball struggles through a turn-of-the-century age of disorder and confusion that may or may not signify its demise as the national pastime, its postmodern narratives have added comic rage to baseball's outrageous conduct by creating a carnivalesque baseball world plagued by subverted traditions and collapsing boundaries and populated by dunces, deviants, and demons. In the postmodern narrative, baseball's traditional and transformative adage, its recurring appeal to its devoted and forgiving fans to wait until next year, has been debunked and redefined as either a meaningless joke, a mocking taunt, or a caustic warning to the postmodern baseball reader that things may get even worse.

MILLER, SAN FRANCISCO, P. C. L

◆ 10 ◆

In Defense of Baseball Books

With all the hoopla surrounding the various lists of the hundred greatest players of the twentieth century, it's easy to overlook the absence of baseball's greatest books from the Modern Library's one hundred best fiction and one hundred best nonfiction lists. No baseball book, according to the distinguished panel of judges, was worthy of a place among the millennium's best fiction and nonfiction.

Yet, as popular as baseball has been in the twentieth century, it's hardly surprising that the game, despite the Modern Library shutout, turns up in several of the century's best books. Thanks to F. Scott Fitzgerald's *The Great Gatsby* and William Faulkner's *The Sound and the Fury,* ranked second and sixth on the best fiction list, baseball actually makes two appearances in the top ten. In *The Great Gatsby,* moral-minded Nick Carraway is staggered when Jay Gatsby tells him Meyer Wolfsheim, modeled after the real-life gangster Arnold Rothstein, has played with the faith of fifty million Americans by fixing the 1919 World Series. In *The Sound and the Fury,* a paranoid Jason

Compson, when asked if he's got his money on the Yankees after their Murderer's Row year of 1927, says there's no way he'd bet on any team with "that fellow Ruth" on it.

Baseball makes an even more substantial appearance on the fiction list at twenty-nine with the Studs Lonigan trilogy. James T. Farrell, who wanted to play second base for the Chicago White Sox more than he wanted to write novels, uses the ballpark as an escape from the tough life on the streets. The ballpark is where the doomed Studs can imagine himself "driving a home run over the center fielder's head and then making one-handed and shoe-string catches in the outfield." Baseball plays close to the same role in Philip Roth's *Portnoy's Complaint* and J. D. Salinger's *The Catcher in the Rye,* ranked at fifty-two and sixty-four. The disordered mind of Alexander Portnoy finds relief only when he remembers the self-assurance and self-control he felt playing center field—"Oh, to be a center fielder, a center fielder—and nothing more." Neurotic Holden Caulfield, who likes Ring Lardner stories, cherishes the baseball mitt of his dead brother Allie and the poems written on it so Allie would "have something to read when he was in the field and nobody was at bat." W. P. Kinsella became so infatuated with this yearning for a lost innocence in *The Catcher in the Rye* that he kidnapped J. D. Salinger for the plot of *Shoeless Joe,* perhaps the most sentimental and nostalgic novel ever written about baseball-loving sons and fathers.

E. L. Doctorow's *Ragtime,* listed at eighty-six, manages to weave the traditional father-son visit to the ballpark into its rich tapestry of turn-of-the century America, but the brief appearance of McGraw's Giants serves only to reinforce the rowdiness of America at the time. The book closest to baseball fiction steps in at ninety-two with William Kennedy's Pulitzer Prize–winning *Ironweed,* a novel about an ex-major-league ballplayer, fashioned after Kennedy's great-uncle Ed McDonald, who played with Boston and Chicago in the American League from 1911 to 1913. Kennedy's ex-ballplayer, a strong-armed, sure-handed third basemen, "a damn fieldin' machine," is, however, a derelict who ruined his career and life when he killed a railway scab with a perfectly thrown rock and later fatally dropped his infant son after an afternoon of drinking beer at a local bar. In *Ironweed,* baseball is mostly a haunting embellishment, a trunk filled with faded clippings and photos and "the odor of lost time." There's no field of dreams in Kennedy's nightmarish Albany, no reconciliation in a game of catch. The novel ends with Francis Phelan on the run again, this time after using a baseball bat to kill a raider at a hobo camp.

Baseball fares even worse on the Modern Library's one hundred best nonfiction list, though there are some close calls. Stephen Jay Gould has written frequently about baseball, including essays on the myth of Cooperstown and the extinction of the .400 hitter, but none of his baseball essays appear in *The Mismeasure of Man,* ranked at twenty-four. In *An American Childhood,* Annie Dillard has written lyrically about her ballplaying, tomboy days while growing up in Pittsburgh and her love affair with the 1960 miracle Pirates, but it's *Pilgrim at Tinker's Creek* that makes the list at eighty-nine. Baseball does, however, get in at fifty-four with Studs Terkel's *Working.* Terkel, who played Chicago baseball writer Hugh Fullerton in the movie version of Eliot Asinof's *Eight Men Out,* included journeyman pitcher Steve Hamilton among three athletes, four if you count the jockey, in the Sporting Life section of *Working.* But Hamilton, one of over 120 individuals interviewed, plays as small a role in Terkel's oral history of working life in America as he did in baseball history.

One reason for the exclusion of baseball books from the lists of the millennium's best fiction and nonfiction is painfully obvious—the Modern Library judges didn't think there was a baseball book published in the twentieth century that was worth putting on either list. But the reasons why the judges didn't find or even consider a baseball book out of the thousands published over the past hundred years may be another matter. It's entirely possible, perhaps even likely, that baseball books, because of their subject, were simply written off or ignored. The judges may have decided that baseball, like Andy Warhol's can of Campbell's tomato soup, is not much more than an artifact of popular culture, a national pastime perhaps, but at best a cultural, social, and historical lightweight, hardly the right stuff for serious writers.

They may also have regarded baseball writers, even at their best, as mere journalists, not much more than literary hacks turning out ephemera to satisfy a reading audience with the attention span of an adolescent. Of the close to fifty sportswriters honored at the Hall of Fame as recipients of the J. G. Taylor Spink Award "for meritorious contributions to baseball writing," only two, Ring Lardner and Damon Runyon, have literary reputations, although neither is regarded as a serious writer by most critics. In his lifetime, Lardner was chastised by F. Scott Fitzgerald for wasting his talent writing about sports. As for the Hall of Fame, it has a national library annexed to the main building, but there is no special room, like the gallery for baseball paintings, or even a window display or bookcase in baseball's shrine for honoring baseball's greatest books.

Yet, while there is no place for baseball's best books on the Modern Library's lists and no hallowed spot at the Hall of Fame, the conventional arguments for dismissing baseball writing because of its content or its form don't hold up very well even within the loftiest literary circle of modern criticism. Henry James, who probably didn't know baseball from cricket but has two novels on the Modern Library's best fiction list, argued in his celebrated essay "The Art of Fiction" that writers should be free to choose their own subject matter and should be judged by how they write, not what they write about. He regarded a writer's freedom as the central principle of literary criticism. James's own fiction was attacked for being insignificant and boring because he wrote in a highly mannered style about the refined world of the European upper class. H. G. Wells once wrote that reading a Henry James novel was like watching a hippopotamus trying to pick up a pea.

Virginia Woolf, whose books appear on the Modern Library's one hundred best fiction and nonfiction lists, reinforced and extended James's argument in her own critical writing by claiming games as a valid and, for American writers, essential subject matter. Unlike sports-minded Fitzgerald, Woolf, who had no real interest in American games, admired Ring Lardner's stories in *You Know Me Al*—Lardner "writes the best prose that has come our way"—and believed that his "interest in games has solved one of the most difficult problems of the American writer; it has given him a clue, a centre, a meeting place for the diverse activities of people whom a vast continent isolates, whom no tradition controls. Games give him what society gives his English brother."

There's a touch of English snobbery in Woolf's attitude toward American writers, but she did recognize that games, especially baseball, would play a defining role for American culture in the twentieth century, that Jacques Barzun would be right in claiming that "whoever wants to learn the heart and mind of America had better learn baseball." But the rub is that America's best writers in the twentieth century, even with the freedom to choose their own subject matter, seldom wrote seriously about baseball. Fitzgerald found a cameo role in *The Great Gatsby* for the 1919 Black Sox scandal, but the writer who ridiculed Lardner for wasting his talent on "a boy's game" was hardly of a mind to write a serious baseball novel. Faulkner, obsessed with the South's defeat in the Civil War, turned mad Jason Compson into a baseball Yankee-hater, but the South would have to wait a few more generations before baseball would come marching into Georgia. Hemingway, in *The Old Man and the Sea,* turned his fisherman into a Joe DiMaggio fan, but Hemingway was much more of an aficionado of bullfighting, big-game hunting, and deep-sea fishing.

There are at least a few major novelists, like Bernard Malamud, who have written serious baseball fiction and one, Philip Roth, who actually has a book on the twentieth century's best fiction list, though obviously not his baseball novel, ironically titled *The Great American Novel.* And there have been works of nonfiction, ranging from histories to biographies, from memoirs to fan books, that have added to our understanding of the forces shaping American culture and society by focusing on the influence of baseball on American society in the twentieth century. Some of these works are so well wrought they've been praised by book critics, recognized as notable books, and nominated for prizes as lofty as the Pulitzer.

If some dedicated twenty-first century reader, with at least a passing interest in baseball, tries to work his or her way through the Modern Library's lists and discovers that James Joyce's *Finnegans Wake*, at seventy-seven on the best fiction list, is unreadable without a critical guide and William Butler Yeats's *Autobiographies*, at thirty-nine on the nonfiction list, is so ponderous and esoteric the book proves that Yeats as a prose writer was a great poet, then he or she might want to take a break and read one of baseball's best books of the twentieth century. What follows is a list of nine baseball books, all, I believe, worthy of consideration for any list of the twentieth century's best fiction or nonfiction. But reader beware—if you read one baseball book, you may want to read another and another, before returning to the Modern Library's lists and Rudyard Kipling's *Kim* or Joseph Needham's *Science and Civilization in China*. And you may even decide that one of these baseball books belongs somewhere among the best of the twentieth century.

A Modest Proposal for Baseball's Greatest Nine

The Natural

There are several outstanding baseball novels—Asinof's *Man on Spikes*, Coover's *The Universal Baseball Association, Inc., J. Henry Waugh, Prop.*, Greenberg's *The Celebrant*, Harris's *Bang the Drum Slowly*, Kinsella's *Shoeless Joe*, Roth's *The Great American Novel*—but Bernard Malamud's *The Natural*, first published in 1952, is the most studied and historically the most important. As to Mark Harris's complaint that *The Natural*, with its mythic scaffolding, isn't baseball, the obvious response is that the best baseball writing is often about the game as dream, even when the dreamer fails.

You Know Me Al

Baseball has been well served by the art of the storyteller—there are wonderful collections of short stories and delightful anthologies of baseball writing, especially *The Fireside Book of Baseball,* edited by Charles Einstein, and *The Armchair Book of Baseball,* edited by John Thorn—but the best spinner of baseball yarns is Ring Lardner. *You Know Me Al,* published in 1916, gave American literature one of its most original characters since Huck Finn floated down the Mississippi. The Jack Keefe stories are a delightful reminder of the richness of the American vernacular and the wonderful comic possibilities in a children's game taken seriously by adults.

The Glory of Their Times

Oral histories have become so much a part of the fabric of baseball's culture and history and produced such a glut of baseball books that some writers and critics have pleaded for a moratorium, perhaps out of fear that the next book will be an oral history of oral historians. Lawrence S. Ritter's *The Glory of Their Times,* published in 1966, is the book that set the standard for oral histories, with its wonderful evocation of the spirit of a nearly lost baseball era through the voices and memories of those who played and loved the game.

The Boys of Summer

One of the complaints about baseball literature is that so much of it is not well written, that love of baseball seldom inspires great writing about the game. Roger Kahn's *The Boys of Summer,* published in 1971, is one of baseball's best-written books. Its carefully and intricately crafted narrative of Kahn's baseball life as a fan and writer and the lives past and present of the Brooklyn Dodgers of the early fifties is one of baseball's most compelling stories. If one baseball book should be on the millennium list this is it.

A False Spring

In a literary landscape cluttered with "as-told-to" books, Pat Jordan's *A False Spring*, published in 1975, is that rare baseball autobiography actually written by its author. It is also one of baseball's best-written and most compelling books, possessed by a frank narrative of the failure of the baseball phenom to live up to his remarkable talent and realize his dream of becoming one of baseball's greatest pitchers.

Babe: The Legend Comes to Life

The baseball biography is another subgenre that has flooded the market. In the case of baseball's most legendary and controversial players there are usually several biographies, ranging from books for children to definitive works. It should come as no surprise that Babe Ruth has been the subject of numerous biographies, but the standard for works on Ruth and for baseball biographies in general is Robert W. Creamer's *Babe: The Legend Comes to Life*, published in 1974, a book remarkable for getting at the truth behind baseball's greatest legend.

Eight Men Out

The Black Sox scandal, the dark cloud hanging over baseball history since the fixing of the 1919 World Series, has provoked numerous historical accounts and inspired several historical novels. Eliot Asinof's *Eight Men Out*, published in 1963, is the seminal work on the scandal and, with its rich detail and compelling story, one of baseball's most impressive narratives, a history written as a novel.

The Pitch That Killed

There have been many books written about baseball's greatest accomplishments—its great eras, great seasons, great performances, and great events—but one of baseball's best books was written about the game's greatest tragedy, Carl Mays's fatal beaning of Ray Chapman during the 1920 season. Mike Sowell's *The Pitch That Killed,* published in 1989, tells the remarkable story of star-crossed ballplayers, so different in temperament and personality but now forever linked in history and legend as baseball's athlete dying young and its irredeemable villain.

Willie's Time

Occasionally, a baseball book, like *The Boys of Summer,* combines several narratives to great effect. Charles Einstein's *Willie's Time,* published in 1979, is subtitled *A Memoir,* but it was nominated for the Pulitzer Prize as a biography. The book is both Einstein's baseball memoir and his biography of Willie Mays, but it places both lives and careers within the context of several decades of American history—from the postwar years of Truman and Eisenhower's fabulous fifties, through the civil rights struggles during the Kennedy and Johnson administrations, to the Vietnam era and the downfall of Nixon.

◆ 11 ◆

How to Write a True Baseball Story

LIVELY, OAKLAND, P. C. L.

Now you can't look it up, but, if you've read enough baseball fiction, you know it's not that easy to write a true baseball story. I'm sure lots of writers have tried, but when they sit down something strange must possess them. Instead of writing truthful things about baseball, they always end up writing fairy tales, ghost stories, or moral romances, but rarely, if ever, do they write a true baseball story.

I'm not going to lie and tell you I've actually written a true baseball story, but I am going to tell the truth about what happened to me when I tried to write a true baseball story. And maybe my true account will explain why it's so hard to write the truth about baseball.

This is not an easy thing to talk about, but as soon as I started to write a true baseball story, I began hearing voices. Now I admit to reading about the voices in *Shoeless Joe,* and I'll even confess to weeping every time I watch the ending of *Field of Dreams,* but this business of hearing voices didn't happen to me in an Iowa cornfield or at a major-league ballpark or at the Hall of Fame. And it didn't happen at midnight in the clear, cool air after a thunderstorm or at noon on a blazing summer day or in some dusk or dawn fog bank. It happened at either ten minutes to ten or ten minutes after ten on an early March Saturday morning or, to be as truthful as I can be, on a March 6 Saturday morning.

I'd like to be more precise about the time, but my wife, depending upon her current outlook on life, sets all the clocks in our house either ten minutes fast or ten minutes slow. I know it was Saturday morning, because that's the only time I have for writing a true baseball story. You see, I'm an English professor, actually a specialist on Irish writers like James Joyce, so during the week I'm too busy playing the academic game. But on Saturday morning, my wife, the retired school teacher, takes off just before nine for her part-time job as a kennel girl at the local vet's office, my son, the eternal college student, is sleeping off his Friday-night poker game with his buddies, and I get to spend some uninterrupted time, or so I thought, writing a true baseball story. And I know the date was March 6, because I checked the *Play Ball* calendar in my study for a good omen, and there it was— March 6 is the birthday of Willie Stargell, one of my favorite players from my childhood team, the Pittsburgh Pirates.

Now when I finally sat down at my desk, I thought about writing a thinly disguised autobiographical story about playing catch with my ghostly father, or maybe going to my first major-league baseball game with my lovingly remembered father, or just talking baseball about my beloved Pirates with my wise and caring father, but I had a hard time figuring out my first sentence. I considered starting my story with "river run past Three Rivers Stadium," but that seemed entirely too Joycean, and "stately, plump Willie Stargell" seemed true but unkind. Finally I had an inspiration, but when I wrote down "Once upon a green field of the mind when I was a boy of summer," an opening sure to catch the eye of Roger Angell of *The New Yorker* or George Plimpton of *The Paris Review,* I heard a voice say:

"If you stop it, he will come."

Obviously, I was surprised by the voice, but I'd have been more in awe if the voice hadn't been so rude and insulting. Besides, at my advanced age, any indicator that you can still hear is a good sign, even if what you hear is a disembodied voice telling you to stop writing. Since I felt more humiliated than honored, I decided to make sure I wasn't confused by the message. After all, the voice, which, by the way, sounded a lot like David McCullough's, might have said, "if you don't stop it, he will come." So I picked up my pen with the miniature Pirate cap on the clicker and, just to make sure, went back to finishing the sentence I thought I'd begun so gloriously. But just as I added "my father and I" to the sentence, I heard a low moan, then the voice spoke again:

"Ease his pain. Don't finish the sentence."

From the desperate and pleading tone of the voice, I knew I had the advantage as long as I had my pen in hand, so I wrote on my Pirate note pad, "if you don't want me to finish the sentence, then tell me who he is and where I can find him." This time, in a tone so angry I thought it would wake the dead, or at least my dead-to-the-world son, the voice thundered out:

"Go the distance. Put down that silly pen,
walk out to your son's car, and go
the distance to the university library.
He'll be in the stacks waiting for you."

As difficult as it is for an English professor to turn his back on a sentence fragment, I got up from my desk, carefully stepped around my cardboard cutout replica of Forbes Field, and hurried out to my son's car. I realized, once I headed up Old U.S. Highway 51, that I should have asked the voice for more specific information. Unlike many of my students and more than a few administrators, I know the location of our library, but I didn't have the exact location in the library for my meeting. The voice had also avoided identifying the mysterious "he," who was, I assume, to be my guide to the true baseball story.

Being a critic by profession, I also wondered why I couldn't just meet my guide at the university's baseball field. Our baseball Salukis were off playing at a tournament somewhere in Florida, Abe Martin Field was deserted, and the morning, for early March, was sunny and pleasant. But here I was, driving by a field with green grass, no lights, and uncomfortable bleacher seats, and instead of meeting Joe Jackson or, better yet, Honus Wagner or Pie Traynor, I had to go to the library for a workshop on how to write a true baseball story.

When I arrived at Morris Library, I discovered that the baseball field wasn't the only place deserted on a Saturday morning. As I walked through the empty main lobby with all the former university presidents staring down at me from their portraits—and not one of them, I should add, wearing a baseball cap—I figured that whoever "he" was, he'd most likely be waiting for me by the library's stacks of baseball books in the recreation division on the fourth floor. I took the stairs instead of the elevator for fear that no one would hear my desperate and pleading voice if the elevator broke down, but when I got to the fourth floor there was no one in sight. I walked in and out of the aisles of books willing to instruct me on everything from mountain climbing to scuba diving, but when I got to the shelves of baseball books, there was no ghost writer waiting to instruct me on the art of writing a true baseball story.

It appeared that my guide wasn't to be some baseball writer skilled in the alchemy of turning the exaggerated anecdotes of old-time players into histories of golden ages and legendary heroes, or even some paleontologist, political commentator, or middle-aged poet claiming to know all about baseball and the meaning of life. The only other possibility, and the one I should have thought of as soon as the voice told me to go the distance to the university library, was that my guide to writing a true baseball story was himself a writer of baseball stories. Who else but a writer of fiction would know how to write the truth about baseball?

As soon as I made my way back down to the humanities division on the second floor, I found the section for American fiction and started walking alphabetically through the stacks. There was no one lurking anywhere from A to Z in the section for nineteenth-century American fiction, but I didn't think that some dime novelist like the creator of Frank Merriwell and his fabulous double-shoot pitch was likely to be my guide for writing a true baseball story. It wasn't until I began moving past the stacks for twentieth-century American fiction that I finally sensed an emanation, and that emanation, to my horror, appeared to be coming from the aisle for authors from K to L. As I turned into the aisle, I was afraid my baseball dream was about to be transformed into a nightmare, that my guide to the true baseball story was to be none other than W. P. Kinsella, the self-proclaimed hater of all academic critics. It was Kinsella, after all, who had said academic critics have no sex life and get their thrills from hunting sexual symbols in literature. It was the same Kinsella who said academics exceed garbage men in pettiness and small-mindedness, a comment I thought rather offensive to garbage men, and had declared that if you truly wanted to be a writer, you should get as far away from academia as possible. I dreaded to think what Kinsella, who said he had the heart of a critic in a jar on his desk, would say to an academic critic who'd decided he should be the one to write a true baseball story.

True enough, my ghost writer or guiding spirit or whatever he was suppose to be was standing in the aisle right by the Ks, but I knew in a moment that what turned to face me was no Buffalo Bill Kinsella in faded denim. My baseball guide, with his straw boater in hand, was a Dapper Dan, tall, clean-shaven, well groomed, and dressed meticulously in a dark suit and tie slightly embellished, to tell the truth, by a bright-striped shirt with a high starched collar. He was certainly no country rube in appearance, though, as fashionable as he looked, his dress was also about eighty years out of date for our meeting.

As I moved down the aisle, I identified myself, but when I reached the Ls and tried to compliment his baseball stories, he stopped me midsentence:

"Let's cut the gab. I know who you are, what you are, and what you've been up to. Why do you think I'm stuck here, staring at my own misbegotten books. And don't give me that hearts-and-flowers routine about my baseball stories. If I hadn't written all that Dear Al stuff, I wouldn't be spending my afterlife traveling through time warps just to baby-sit another rook who thinks he can write a true baseball story. Do you have any idea of how many of you are out there, thinking you know all about baseball, all writing the same lies about your ballplaying youth, all telling the same boring stories about your poor dead fathers, and not knowing enough to fill a knothole about playing baseball or writing fiction?

"Well, don't just stand there looking sheepish and forlorn. I'm not exactly remembered for my kind words or goodness of heart, you know. Besides, I've got more than one rook on my lineup card today, and I'm not getting any relief help. If you want to know how to write a true baseball story—and why anyone in his right mind would want to write a true baseball story is beyond me—let's find a corner somewhere so I can set you straight."

I was beginning to feel more haunted than helped and, I confess, more than a little curious about a couple of the complaints from my Hall of Fame writer, but I let things go for the moment. I suggested we walk up the aisles to the rare book room, a place rarely visited even on weekdays. Fortunately, when we entered the reception area there was no one on duty, so we stepped into the small workroom and sat down at one of the tables.

"This place looks like a mausoleum. Just look at all the busts in here. There's D. H. Lawrence and G. B. Shaw and James Joyce, all looking down at you and me, and we're going to talk about writing baseball stories. Why don't you just write something critical about baseball fiction—there's my sorry attempts at short stories, and the copycat stuff by Runyon and Thurber, and there's Harris's Horatio Alger stuff, and Kinsella's fairy tales. Why not just write an essay about the way baseball writers keep feeding adolescent hooey to all those Huck Finns and Holden Caufields out there who never want to grow up. It wasn't Abner Doubleday who invented baseball. It was Peter Pan."

I got up from the table, picked up a scratch sheet from the top of the card catalog, sat back down, and began copying out the unfinished first sentence of my baseball story.

"Alright, I got the message. So let's get this over and done with. First of all, if you want to write a baseball story readers are going to think is true then get your baseball details right and maybe mix in a little history—but lay off the Black Sox stuff because that's been done to death and, besides, that fellow Asinof already proved the real story is better than fiction. You maybe can throw in some real-life players just for fun, but then you've still got to think about your main character. You've got nine positions, unless you're dumb enough to write about a manager or, worse yet, an umpire, but I'd say stay with a pitcher when you're starting out because he's the center of attention anyway. All you need to do is come up with a colorful nickname, maybe something a little better than Lefty or Cannonball, a larger-than-life personality, maybe exaggerate his size or shrink his intelligence, and make him a green rookie trying to prove himself or a washed-up vet trying to show that he still belongs. Pitch your character in the pennant- or World Series–deciding game, and what do you have—a baseball story."

As I sat there trying hard not to stare at the straw boater on the table and even harder not to lose my patience, I realized I had just been fed a lot of hooey. My ghost writer was giving me clichés and formulas instead of telling me how to write a true baseball story. Instead of playing along, I decided to go after him. I challenged him to stop his griping about rook writers and Peter Pan readers and for once in his life, or at least in his afterlife, tell a true baseball story.

"So you want the truth about baseball and you want it in a story. No boobs or rubes. No naturals or supernaturals. No fields of dreams. No fathers playing catch with sons. No two outs in the bottom of the ninth, bases loaded, three-two counts, no let's win the pennant or World Series for little Bobby or Billy in the hospital. Just the truth. Well, let's see how you handle this one.

"A long time ago, when the game really mattered, there were three boys, let's call them brothers, who loved baseball. Now the first brother had a real passion for playing the game. He wasn't that powerful or that fast, but he was so determined to be the best that he was a demon on the field. Winning was so important to him that he was willing to do anything in a game to give himself the edge. He became feared and even hated, but no one was better at winning a baseball game.

"The second brother was a gifted ballplayer, a natural, but unlike the first brother, who was willing to play anywhere just to win, the second brother always pitched, because he knew that if he pitched, he could control the game. He was a great pitcher, but his real passion was for organizing and controlling things. He kept all the equipment, scheduled all the games, and made up all the rules. He insisted on telling everyone when to bat and where to play. He was resented and distrusted, but if anyone complained or wouldn't play by the rules, the second brother would just pick up his bats and balls and threaten to go home.

"The third brother, unlike the other two, wasn't much of a ballplayer, but he loved baseball with a true passion for the game. He admired the skill and talent of his brothers and enjoyed watching them play so much that he invented statistics to keep a record of what they accomplished on the field and even wrote up summaries and stories about each game. He was always the last one picked, if he were picked at all, but he didn't mind as long as he could watch his brothers play the game and keep a record of their glory and their greatness.

"Now, I'd like to tell you that the three brothers lived happily ever after. After all, they loved the game of baseball and each, according to his own passion, became successful and famous. But you wanted a true baseball story, so here's what really happened. To tell the truth, the first brother, who played the game with a fierce and ruthless passion for winning, became frustrated and resentful when he realized that the people who started coming out to watch the games didn't really appreciate or enjoy his way of playing baseball. They applauded his daring and cunning, but what truly excited and thrilled them was the long ball. So to win the fans' adulation, he changed into a home-run hitter, but, as the fans cheered his epic slugging, he lost his hunger for playing the game as well as his passion for winning.

"When the second brother saw all the people coming out to watch his first brother's heroics, he decided to start charging admission. Once he realized how much money there was in baseball, he quit playing the game, though he was still in his prime, and became a magnate. Eventually he turned baseball into a business monopoly by making all the equipment and creating his own teams and leagues. He even figured out a way to own all the players and control their salaries, though when he saw the way the fans worshipped the home run he made sure the long-ball hitters were publicly honored and celebrated as heroes though not necessarily well paid as ballplayers.

"The third brother, the one who most truly loved baseball, became disheartened when he saw his first brother's passion for winning become a desire for popularity and fame and his second brother's passion for success become a lust for money and power. He watched the playing of the game become less skillful and its management more selfish and greedy. As baseball became less enjoyable and interesting as a pastime, he grew bitter and cynical and even took to drinking too much as he watched the games. When he wrote about baseball, he mocked his first brother's larger-than-life reputation and ridiculed his second brother's moral hypocrisy. Finally he became so bored with the game he had loved so much that he turned his back on baseball, staggered away from the ballpark, and lived unhappily ever after."

My guide to the true baseball story got up from the table, picked up his straw boater, but before he left he offered me some final advice:

"Now that I've told you a true baseball story, maybe you can see now why it's probably better if you just forget about writing the truth about baseball. Most of us can only take so much of the truth, and when it comes to baseball, we usually can't take much truth at all. But you decide. If you ever need to hear from me again, there's always my books out on the shelves. The only thing I ask is that you think about what I've told you before you sit down again with that God awful sentence—'Once upon a green field of the mind when I was a boy of summer, my father and I. . . .' What a lot of hooey. You're lucky all you got was a visit from a washed up, cynical baseball writer and not a Judge Kenesaw Mountain Landis ready to ban you forever from writing another word about baseball."

After my ghost writer waved his boater in farewell, he sauntered out of the rare book room and faded into the shelves. Once he was gone, I got up from the table and quickly made my way out of the library to the parking lot. As I drove home, I tried to make some sense out of what I had just seen and heard. There was, of course, the obvious conclusion that after all the years of reading literature, including an unhealthy amount of James Joyce and baseball fiction, I was finally stricken by delusions and needed psychiatric help or, at least, a heavy dose of Russian realism to purge my soul. Yet, there was also a slim possibility that, delusions or not, my voices and spirits had left behind some lingering truth about writing a baseball story, though instead of feeling as if I'd just completed some magical adventure in search of baseball's Golden Fleece or Holy Grail, I felt left behind and disillusioned. I'd encountered a reluctant baseball guide who appeared before me as if he were paying some terrible penance for having used his talent to write baseball stories. I'd listened to his true baseball story turn into a bitter parable about the betrayal of baseball by those most responsible for loving and taking care of the game. And, worst of all, after going the distance, I was told I could ease everyone's pain by forgetting about writing a true baseball story because nobody wants to hear the truth about baseball.

When I got home, I went right to my study and slumped down at my desk. I took out my Pirate pen and, to the sound of a disembodied sigh of relief, I crossed out my unfinished sentence. As I sat there, I looked around at all my baseball artifacts until I came to my *Play Ball* calendar—and there he was. At the end of a long list of ballplayers born on March 6, including Lefty Grove, my Willie Stargell, and even one-armed Pete Gray, was Ringgold "Ring" Lardner, 1885, *Chicago Tribune* sportswriter. I figured, what the hell, nobody's going to believe me anyway, so I wrote down, to the sound of distant grumblings, the first sentence to a true baseball story:

"Now you can't look it up, but, if you've read enough baseball fiction, you know it's not that easy to write a true baseball story."

Works Cited

Alexander, Charles C. *Our Game: An American Baseball History*. New York: Henry Holt, 1991.

———. *Rogers Hornsby*. New York: Henry Holt, 1995.

———. *Ty Cobb*. New York: Oxford University Press, 1984.

Alpine, Gordon. *Joy in Mudville*. New York: Dutton, 1989.

Angell, Roger. "The Interior Stadium" (1971). In *The Armchair Book of Baseball II*. Ed. John Thorn. New York: Scribner's, 1987. 17–25

Ardizzone, Tony. *Heart of the Order*. New York: Holt, 1986.

Asinof, Eliot. *The Bedfellow*. New York: Simon and Shuster, 1967.

———. *Eight Men Out: The Black Sox and the 1919 World Series*. 1963. Reprint, New York: Henry Holt, 1987.

———. *Man on Spikes*. New York: McGraw-Hill, 1955.

Barzun, Jacques. *God's Country and Mine*. New York: Vintage, 1954.

Beckham, Barry. *Runner Mack*. New York: Morrow, 1972.

Bjarkman, Peter C. Introduction to *Baseball and the Game of Life*. Ed. Peter C. Bjarkman. New York: Random House, 1991. ix–xxii.

Boswell, Thomas. *Cracking the Show*. New York: Doubleday, 1994.

———. *How Life Imitates the World Series*. New York: Doubleday, 1982.

———. *Why Time Begins on Opening Day*. New York: Doubleday, 1984.

Bouton, Jim. *Ball Four*. Ed. Leonard Shecter. 1970. Reprint, New York: Macmillan, 1990.

Boyd, Brendan. *Blue Ruin: A Novel of the 1919 World Series*. New York: Norton, 1991.

Boyle, T. Coraghessan. "The Hector Quesadilla Story" (1986). In *Baseball's Best Short Stories*. Ed. Paul D. Staudohar. Chicago: Chicago Review Press, 1995. 375–87.

Brashler, William. *The Bingo Long Traveling All-Stars and Motor Kings: A Novel*. 1973. Reprint, Urbana: University of Illinois Press, 1993.

Brock, Darryl. *If I Never Get Back*. New York: Crown, 1990.

Brosnan, Jim. *The Long Season*. New York: Harper, 1960.

Buck, Ashley. "A Pitcher Grows Tired" (1946). In *Baseball's Best Short Stories*. Ed. Paul D. Staudohar. Chicago: Chicago Review Press, 1995. 173–78.

Canin, Ethan. "City of Broken Hearts." In *The Palace Thief: Stories*. New York: Random House, 1994. 107–51.

Carkeet, David. *The Greatest Slump of All Time*. New York: Harper, 1984.

Chabon, Michael. "Smoke" (1990). In *Baseball's Best Short Stories*. Ed. Paul D. Staudohar. Chicago: Chicago Review Press, 1995. 133–42.

Charyn, Jerome. *The Seventh Babe*. New York: Arbor House, 1979.

Cobb, Ty, with Al Stump. *My Life in Baseball: The True Record*. New York: Doubleday, 1961.

Coover, Robert. "McDuff on the Mound." *Iowa Review* 2.4 (1971): 111–20.

———. *The Universal Baseball Association, Inc., J. Henry Waugh, Prop*. New York: Random House, 1968.

Craig, John. *Chappie and Me*. New York: Dodd, Mead, 1979.

Creamer, Robert W. *Babe: The Legend Comes to Life*. New York: Simon and Shuster, 1974.

DeLillo, Don. "Pafko at the Wall." *Harper's*, October 1992, 35–70.

Dillard, Annie. *An American Childhood*. New York: Harper, 1987.

Doctorow, E. L. *Ragtime*. New York: Random House, 1974.

Dubus, Andre. "The Pitcher" (1979). In *Fielder's Choice*. Ed. Jerome Holtzman. New York: Harcourt Brace, 1980. 349–65.

Duncan, David James. *The Brothers K*. New York: Doubleday, 1992.

Durso, Joseph. *Baseball and the American Dream*. St. Louis: The Sporting News, 1986.

Dybek, Stuart. "Death of a Right Fielder" (1990). In *Baseball's Best Short Stories*. Ed. Paul D. Staudohar. Chicago: Chicago Review Press, 1995. 355–58.

Einstein, Charles, ed. *The Fireside Book of Baseball*. New York: Simon and Shuster, 1956.

Einstein, Charles. *Willie's Time: A Memoir*. Philadelphia: J. B. Lippincott, 1979.

Farrell, James T. *Studs Lonigan Trilogy*. New York: Random House, 1938.

Faulkner, William. *The Sound and the Fury*. 1929. Reprint, New York: Norton, 1994.

Fisher, Leonard Everett. *Noonan: A Novel about Baseball, ESP, and Time Warps*. New York: Doubleday, 1978.

Fitzgerald, Ed. *The Ballplayer*. New York: Barnes, 1957.

Fitzgerald, F. Scott. *The Great Gatsby*. 1925. Reprint, New York: Scribner, 1995.

Frank, Stanley. "The Name of the Game" (1949). In *The Fireside Book of Baseball*. Ed. Charles Einstein. New York: Simon and Shuster, 1956. 134–41.

Giamatti, A. Bartlett. "The Green Fields of the Mind" (1977). In *The Armchair Book of Baseball*. Ed. John Thorn. New York: Scribners, 1985. 141–43.

Goldstein, Warren. "Inside Baseball." *The Gettysburg Review* 5 (1992): 410–22.

Goodwin, Doris Kearns. *Wait till Next Year*. New York: Simon and Shuster, 1998.

Gould, Stephen Jay. "The Creation Myths of Cooperstown." In *Writing Baseball*. Ed. Jerry Klinkowitz. Urbana: University of Illinois Press, 1991. 23–34.

———. "Good Sports and Bad." *New York Review of Books*, March 9, 1995, 20–24.

———. "A Philosophical Conclusion." In *Full House: The Spread of Excellence from Plato to Darwin*. New York: Three Rivers Press, 1996. 129–32.

———. "The Streak of Streaks." *New York Review of Books*, August 18, 1988, 8–12.

———. "Why the Death of 0.400 Hitting Records Improvement of Play." In *Full House: The Spread of Excellence from Plato to Darwin*. New York: Three Rivers Press, 1996. 111–28.

Graham, John Alexander. *Babe Ruth Caught in a Snowstorm*. Boston: Houghton Mifflin, 1973.

Greenberg, Eric Rolfe. *The Celebrant*. 1983. Reprint, New York: Penguin, 1986.

Gregorich, Barbara. *She's on First*. Chicago: Contemporary, 1987.

Hall, Donald. *Fathers Playing Catch with Sons*. San Francisco: North Point, 1985.

Hamill, Peter. *Snow in August*. New York: Little, Brown, 1997.

Hano, Arnold. "The Umpire Was a Rookie" (1956). In *Baseball's Best Short Stories*. Ed. Paul D. Staudohar. Chicago: Chicago Review Press, 1995. 359–74.

Harris, Mark. *Bang the Drum Slowly*. New York: Knopf, 1956.

———. "Bring Back That Old Sandlot Novel." *New York Times Book Review,* October 16, 1988, 44–45.

———. "Horatio at the Bat; or, Why Such a Lengthy Embryonic Period for the Serious Baseball Novel." *Aethlon* 5.2 (1988): 1–11.

———. *It Looked Like Forever*. New York: McGraw-Hill, 1979.

———. *The Southpaw*. Indianapolis: Bobbs-Merrill Co., 1953.

———. *A Ticket for a Seamstitch*. New York: Knopf, 1956.

Hays, Donald. *The Dixie Association*. New York: Simon and Shuster, 1984.

Heinz, W. C. "One Throw" (1950). In *Baseball's Best Short Stories*. Ed. Paul D. Staudohar. Chicago: Chicago Review Press, 1995. 143–48.

Helyar, John. *Lords of the Realm: The Real History of Baseball*. New York: Mass Market, 1995.

Hoak, Don, with Myron Cope. "The Day I Batted against Castro" (1964). In *The Armchair Book of Baseball*. Ed. John Thorn. New York: Scribner's, 1985. 161–64.

Hough, John Jr. *The Conduct of the Game*. New York: Harcourt Brace, 1986.

Huizinga, J. *Homo Ludens: A Study of the Play Element in Culture*. Boston: Beacon, 1955.

Jordan, Pat. *A False Spring*. New York: Dodd, Mead, 1975.

Kahn, Roger. *The Boys of Summer*. New York: Harper, 1971.

———. *Good Enough to Dream*. New York: Doubleday, 1985.

———. *The Seventh Game*. New York: New American Library, 1982.

Kennedy, William. *Ironweed*. New York: Viking, 1983.

Kinsella, W. P. *The Dixon Cornbelt League and Other Baseball Stories*. New York: Harper Collins, 1993.

———. Foreword to *Hummers, Knucklers, and Slow Curves: Contemporary Baseball Poems*. Ed. Don Johnson. Urbana: University of Illinois Press, 1991. xvii–xviii.

———. *The Iowa Baseball Confederacy.* Boston: Houghton Mifflin, 1986.

———. *Shoeless Joe.* Boston: Houghton-Mifflin, 1982.

———. *The Thrill of the Grass.* New York: Penguin, 1984.

Klinkowitz, Jerry. *Basepaths.* Baltimore: Johns Hopkins University Press, 1995.

———. Introduction to *Writing Baseball.* Ed. Jerry Klinkowitz. Urbana: University of Illinois Press, 1991. 1–20.

———. *Short Season and Other Stories.* Baltimore: Johns Hopkins University Press, 1988.

Koppett, Leonard. *A Thinking Man's Guide to Baseball.* New York: Dutton, 1967.

Lardner, John. Introduction to *You Know Me Al* (1916), by Ring W. Lardner. New York: Macmillan, 1991. 5–15.

Lardner, Ring W. *Lose with a Smile.* New York: Scribner's, 1933.

———. *You Know Me Al.* 1916. Reprint, Urbana: University of Illinois Press, 1992.

Lasher, Lawrence M. *Conversations with Bernard Malamud.* Jackson: University of Mississippi Press, 1991.

Malamud, Bernard. *The Natural.* New York: Harcourt, Brace, 1952.

———. "Reflections of a Writer: Long Work, Short Life." *New York Times Book Review,* March 20, 1988, 15–18.

Mayer, Robert. *The Grace of Shortstops.* New York: Doubleday, 1984.

Mazza, Chris. "Caught." *Aethlon* 5 (Fall 1988): 13–21.

McManus, James. *Chin Music.* New York: Crown, 1985.

Nauen, Elinor, ed. *Diamonds Are a Girl's Best Friend.* New York: Faber and Faber, 1995.

Neugeboren, Jay. *Sam's Legacy.* New York: Holt, Rinehart, 1973.

Plimpton, George. *The Curious Case of Sidd Finch.* New York: Macmillan, 1987.

Powers, J. F. "Jamesie" (1947). In *Baseball's Best Short Stories.* Ed. Paul D. Staudohar. Chicago: Chicago Review Press, 1995. 283–302.

Quigley, Martin. *The Original Colored House of David.* Boston: Houghton Mifflin, 1981.

———. *Today's Game.* New York: Viking, 1965.

Rader, Benjamin G. *Baseball: A History of America's Game.* Urbana: University of Illinois Press, 1992.

————. Introduction to *America's National Game* (1911), by Albert G. Spalding. Lincoln: University of Nebraska Press, 1992. ix–xv.

Ritter, Lawrence S. *The Glory of Their Times: The Story of the Early Days of Baseball.* 1966. Reprint, New York: William Morrow, 1984.

Roth, Philip. *The Great American Novel.* New York: Holt, Rinehart, 1973.

————. *Portnoy's Complaint.* New York: Random House, 1969.

Runyon, Damon. "Baseball Hattie" (1954). In *Fielder's Choice.* Ed. Jerome Holtzman. New York: Harcourt Brace, 1980. 143–55.

Salinger, J. D. *The Catcher in the Rye.* New York: Little, Brown, 1951.

Sayles, John. *Pride of the Bimbos.* Boston: Little, Brown, 1975.

Seymour, Harold. *Baseball: The Early Years.* New York: Oxford University Press, 1960.

————. *Baseball: The Golden Age.* New York: Oxford University Press, 1971.

————. *Baseball: The People's Game.* New York: Oxford University Press, 1990.

Shannon, Mike. *Diamond Classics: Essays on 100 of the Best Baseball Books Ever Published.* Jefferson, N.C.: McFarland, 1989.

Shepard, Jim. "Batting against Castro" (1993). In *The Best American Short Stories 1994.* Ed. Tobias Wolff and Katrina Kenison. Boston: Houghton, Mifflin, 1994. 277–92, 342–43.

Sowell, Mike. *The Pitch That Killed: Carl Mays, Ray Chapman, and the Pennant Race of 1920.* New York: Macmillan, 1989.

Spalding, Albert G. *America's National Game.* 1911. Reprint, Lincoln: University of Nebraska Press, 1992.

Spink, Alfred H. *The National Game.* St. Louis: National Game Publishing Co., 1911.

Stein, Harry. *Hoopla.* New York: Knopf, 1983.

Stump, Al. *Cobb.* Chapel Hill, N.C.: Algonquin Books, 1996.

Terkel, Studs. *Working.* New York: New Press, 1974.

Thorn, John, ed. *The Armchair Book of Baseball.* New York: Scribner's, 1985.

Thurber, James. "You Could Look It Up" (1941). In *Baseball's Best Short Stories.* Ed. Paul D. Staudohar. Chicago: Chicago Review Press, 1995. 117–32.

Voigt, David Quentin. *American Baseball: From Gentleman's Sport to the Commissioner's System.* Norman: University of Oklahoma Press, 1966.

————. *American Baseball: From the Commissioners to Continental Expansion.* Norman: University of Oklahoma Press, 1970.

————. *American Baseball: From Postwar Expansion to the Electronic Age.* University Park: Pennsylvania State University Press, 1983.

Wallop, Douglass. *The Year the Yankees Lost the Pennant.* New York: Norton, 1954.

Warren, Robert Penn. "Goodwood Comes Back" (1948). In *Baseball's Best Short Stories.* Ed. Paul D. Staudohar. Chicago: Chicago Review Press, 1995. 73–84.

Wasserman, Earl R. "*The Natural:* Malamud's World Ceres." *The Centennial Review* 9 (1965): 438–60.

Watson, Lawrence. "Pinstripe" (1985). In *Baseball and the Game of Life.* Ed. Peter C. Bjarkman. New York: Random House, 1991. 49–65.

Westbrook, Deanne. *Ground Rules: Baseball and Myth.* Urbana: University of Illinois Press, 1996.

White, G. Edward. *Creating the National Pastime: Baseball Transforms Itself, 1903–1953.* Princeton, N.J.: Princeton University Press, 1996.

Will, George F. *Men at Work: The Craft of Baseball.* New York: Macmillan, 1990.

Willard, Nancy. *Things Invisible to See.* New York: Knopf, 1984.

Williams, Ted, with John Underwood. *My Turn at Bat.* New York: Simon and Shuster, 1969.

Winegardner, Mark. *The Veracruz Blues.* New York: Viking, 1996.

Woolf, Virginia. "American Fiction." In *Collected Essays,* vol. 2. New York: Harcourt, Brace, 1967. 111–21.

Index

Richard Peterson, a professor of English at Southern Illinois University at Carbondale, is the editor of the *Crab Orchard Review* and of Southern Illinois University Press's Writing Baseball series. His baseball essays and stories have appeared in the *Chicago Tribune, Creative Nonfiction, Elysian Fields, Nine, Sports Literate, Aethlon,* and other publications, and he has also published books on James Joyce, William Butler Yeats, and Mary Lavin.

Eliot Asinof is renowned among baseball writers for *Eight Men Out: The Black Sox and the 1919 World Series.* He has also written *Man on Spikes, Off-Season,* and other baseball books.

Sport and Society

Making the Team: The Cultural Work of Baseball Fiction *Timothy Morris*
Making the American Team: Sport, Culture, and the Olympic Experience
Mark Dyreson
Viva Baseball! Latin Major Leaguers and Their Special Hunger
Samuel O. Regalado
Touching Base: Professional Baseball and American Culture in the
Progressive Era (rev. ed.) *Steven A. Riess*
Red Grange and the Rise of Modern Football *John M. Carroll*
Golf and the American Country Club *Richard J. Moss*
Extra Innings: Writing on Baseball *Richard Peterson*

Reprint Editions

The Nazi Olympics *Richard D. Mandell*
Sports in the Western World (2d ed.) *William J. Baker*

Composed in 10/14 Sabon
with Flyer Bold Condensed display
by Jim Proefrock
at the University of Illinois Press
Designed by Dennis Roberts
Manufactured by Cushing-Malloy, Inc.

University of Illinois Press
1325 South Oak Street
Champaign, IL 61820-6903
www.press.uillinois.edu